ROYAL FAMILY

ROYAL FAMILY

Finding Your Identity and Purpose in The Kingdom of God

JOHN NICHOLAS PRASSAS
Forward by Leighton Ford

ABBA
PRESS

Palos Verdes, CA 90274

Acknowledgements

My sincere thanks to Margi Emmons for providing an excellent editorial review of this manuscript, complete with many fine suggestions. Thanks also to Evan Kim, Rich Salmon, Rick Kamrath and Julia Anderson for contributing valuable counsel, technical support, artwork and editorial feedback, respectively.

Thanks also to my wife Suzi, for keeping her faith in this project long enough to encourage me, and for keeping the kids out of my office long enough to let me finish!

For information regarding interviews, speaking engagements, etc., call: 1-800-ABBA-957

Scripture quotations are from the *New American Standard Bible (NASB)*, Thomas Nelson Publishers, 1985, the *New International Version (NIV)*, International Bible Society, 1984, or *Today's English Version (TEV)*, American Bible Society, 1966.

Library of Congress Catalog Card Number: 93-90361

International Standard Book Number (ISBN): 0-9636999-0-3

DEDICATED:

To my parents, Bill and Barbara Prassas, who
made this book – and a million other good things – possible.

To my wife Suzi, and to my children, Christina, A.J.,
Adam and Willie, who surround me with love.

To my good friend, Timothy Montgomery,
who confirmed God's presence in my life.

To Dr. Leighton Ford, who clarified
the meaning of vision, integrity and ministry.

To my other family members and friends,
who support me in all my ventures.

And to all who "seek first His kingdom,"
with hopes of dwelling there.

Contents

Forward

As we move toward the 21rst century, I believe God is raising up a group of gifted and devoted young communicators to advance His kingdom – like my friend, John Prassas, who has written this book.

I first met John over lunch in Pasadena, where he was studying at Fuller Seminary. He had written and produced an evangelistic video that was brought to my attention. As I heard his testimony and vision for ministry, I was drawn to him. Later he attended one of our leadership training sessions, and we got to know each other better. And since then, whenever I visit Los Angeles, we try to spend some time together.

As John and I have talked about *Royal Family*, I have encouraged him. Not only because John is a gifted writer, but because the message is so vitally needed. To a generation which constantly hears about "family values" (and often hasn't experienced them), this book should speak powerfully. John has given us a simple, beautiful, biblical and compelling portrait of what it means to belong to a new family, as adopted children of God.

I myself am an adopted son. I've always been grateful that my adopted parents didn't <u>have</u> to love me. They <u>chose</u> to! And what a tremendous affirmation it is to know an even greater truth – that the God of the universe has adopted me – an unworthy sinner – to be His son and servant! Like John, I long for everyone to know this transforming relationship with the living God.

If you're thinking about becoming a Christian, but with hesitations, this book will provide you a clear and attractive description of what it might be like to "belong to God's family," and how to enter it.

If you're a new Christian, you'll find an understanding of God (theology!) that will stabilize, strengthen and teach you about family priviledges, joys and responsibilities.

If you've been in the family awhile, but haven't fully experienced the "love of God shed abroad in your heart through the Holy Spirit" (Rom. 5:5), you'll find pointers to the refreshing, renewing quality of life and community God desires you to know and enjoy. And even if you don't agree with every aspect of John's teaching, you'll still benefit from it.

And if you're trying to bring others into the family, you'll find here both motivation and a model of how to make the invitation of Christ realistic and attractive.

I recommend *Royal Family* warmly, and am thankful that John and I are part of God's family together!

Leighton Ford
Charlotte, North Carolina

Family Ties

"But as many as received Him (Jesus),
to them He gave the right to become
children of God." – John 1:12

"What does it really *mean* to be Christian?" I wondered. "Where do I fit in?" "Who am I??"

I felt guilty asking such questions. But I couldn't help myself. I had been a Christian several years, and was growing more frustrated every day. Something vital was missing in my life, even though, by all appearances, I was a "good Christian."

I served at church, witnessed at work, hosted a fellowship at home. I studied the Bible. I read apologetics. I even wrote evangelism tracts. I learned about Christian financial planning, parenting, schooling and prayer. I experienced the Holy Spirit, too. I was even recognized as an emerging church leader.

But I was still depressed. I still lacked vision for my life. I still couldn't see the big picture, or where I fit in. Sure, I loved God. I had given my life to following Christ. But what did that mean? *Where was I to follow? How* was I to follow? What was I to *do*, while following? I didn't have a clue.

Worse than that, I lacked identity. I knew God had supernaturally made me a "new creature" in Christ, and that "old things had passed away, new things had come."[1] Deep down, I *knew* I was new. I certainly felt new. But a new what? What kind of "new creature" had I become?? I honestly didn't know.

It didn't help matters any to learn that Christians are called *many* things, including "salt," "light," "sheep," "soldiers," "saints," and even members of the "body" a*nd* "bride" of Christ! These metaphors, valuable as they are, only confused me. I still couldn't figure out what – or who – I had become as a Christian.

So I continued to struggle in my Christian "identity crisis," desperate for a vision, dying for a sense of purpose, yearning to break out of my shackles of ignorance. My spirit groaned for a revelation.

Then, one day, it happened. I read Romans 8:15, and it hit me like lightning.

> "You have not received a spirit of slavery leading to fear again, you have received the Spirit of adoption as sons by which we cry out, 'Abba! Father!'"

I was shocked and excited all at once. Could I really be a "son??" Had I really been "adopted??" Did "new creature" really mean child of God?? Confirmation came quickly, through scriptures like John 1:12,

> "But as many as received Him, to them He gave the right to become children of God."

---

[1] II Corinthians 5:14

And I John 3:1,

> "How great is the love the Father has lavished on us, that we should be called children of God! And that is what we are!"

There were many other verses highlighting our "family ties" with God, as well. And I consumed them like a beggar eating bread. But as I digested them, I began to wonder. Had I totally overlooked this vision of life as a "child of God?" Had I missed something so well known it's mentioned in sermons every day? That's when I realized my problem. Because it's so simple and obvious, I had simply taken it for granted.

As Christians, we often hear that we're "children of God." But do we ever stop to explore what that really *means*? Do we dig into the *everyday reality* of that existence? Do we truly grasp our *supernatural status* in God's kingdom? I don't think so. And I think we suffer a form of spiritual poverty, as a result.

I've written this book, based on my own life-changing exploration of this subject, because I think it's time for a change.

I believe it's time to discover the treasure of God's kingdom, of who who we are and how we fit in. I believe it's time to catch a bold vision for our lives as sons and daughters, brothers and sisters, princes and princesses in God's Royal Family.

If you believe the same thing, or are open to the possibilities, then read on – and let His kingdom come!

CHAPTER ONE

The Fallen Family

*"Through one man (Adam) sin entered the world,
and death through sin." – Romans 5:12*

When you were born, did you enter the kingdom of God? Did you become a member of God's family? No, unfortunately, you didn't. Jesus explained that, to enter God's kingdom, you must be "born from above," not of human flesh, but of God's Spirit.[1] The apostle Paul called this spiritual experience "adoption,"[2] a radical change of family membership we'll explore throughout this book.

You *did* enter the world, however, that cruel, unforgiving place, sometimes called "hell on earth." You *did* become a member of Adam's fallen family, that perverted and dysfunctional clan, better known as the human race. You did, indeed, come from "the wrong side of the tracks!"

Why do I say this? Why am I being so negative? Because you need to "face the music" as soon as possible. Because, chances are, you won't seek the wealth and freedom of God's kingdom, until you face the poverty and bondage of the world. You won't accept the "abundant

---

[1] John 3:1-7
[2] Ephesians 1:5, Romans 8:15, etc.

life"[3] offered by Jesus, until you reject its rotten alternative. <u>You won't live as a child of God</u>, <u>until you see the fallen "human condition" for what it really is</u>. And, tragically, *very few Christians do.*

This fact hit home recently, when I read the results of a nationwide survey, which found that 83% of the population – including most Christians – agreed with the statement, "People are basically good." I couldn't believe such nonsense!

What's wrong with saying "people are basically good?" Oh, nothing if you don't mind ignoring daily reports of war, murder, corruption, and child molestation. Nothing, if you don't mind denying the oppression, exploitation, rape, torture, deception, theft and slander that fill the pages of history. Nothing, if you don't mind living in fantasyland!

You see, it's one thing to say that people are occasionally good, or that people want to be good. We all have good intentions, and good moments. We all have good qualities, too. But to say that people are "basically good" just doesn't wash with the heart-breaking facts of life. It doesn't even square with our own experience, which tells us people are basically selfish, jealous and even dangerous!

So why deceive ourselves with wishful thinking? Why deny the obvious? People are NOT basically good.

What are people, then, if not "basically good?" Well, the truth is, <u>people are basically sinful</u>. The Bible says, "There is not a righteous person on earth who continually

---

[3] John 10:10

does good and never sins,"[4] and that, "All have sinned and fall short of the glory of God."[5]   King David of Israel confessed, "Surely I was sinful at birth, sinful from the time my mother conceived me."[6] And surely, you and I can say the same thing.

How did we get into this mess? What does it mean to be sinful? What are the symptoms of our condition? To understand, we need to trace our family tree – all the way back to its "roots" in the garden of Eden.

DOUBT IN THE GARDEN

The Bible's story of Adam and Eve reveals the truth of our human condition like nothing else on earth.   It tells us that people were *originally* good.

As part of God's good creation, Adam and Eve were totally approved in God's sight. In fact, they were created in the very "image of God."[7]   This meant they were a *reflection* of God. Their identity was found in spiritual relationship with Him. Their responsibility to care for the earth, along with their high levels of intelligence, freedom and creativity, all came from Him.

Life in the garden was characterized by "Shalom," the Hebrew word for peace, or wholeness. Adam and Eve lacked nothing. They enjoyed God's presence and fellowship, as well as God's provision for all their needs. They enjoyed unity and security together. Their life was simple

---

[4] Ecclesiastes 7:20
[5] Romans 3:23
[6] Psalm 51:5
[7] Genesis 1:27

and peaceful. In short, *they enjoyed a life of harmony with God and with each other*. Can you imagine such harmony? It was heaven on earth.

Paradise was lost however, when Adam and Eve ate from the tree of knowledge, an act forbidden by God, under penalty of death. Their disobedience was provoked by a serpent (Satan) who mocked God's justice ("Of course you won't die!" he insisted), and challenged God's intentions ("He doesn't want you to be wise like Him, that's all!" he argued). He tempted them to become "like God."[8] Tragically, they fell for his lies, ate the forbidden fruit and thus committed the original sin.

What does "sin" actually mean? Sin is rebellion against God. It's the rejection of His protection and care. It's disobedience toward His simple commands. And the *result* of sin is perversion. That is, sin *distorts* humanity, making people less than God intended, flawed, defective, and ultimately bent toward destruction and death. Sin seperates us from God. Sin seperates us from each other. And sin seperates us from our true selves. In short, sin ruins everything!

What's the root *cause* of sin? This is important to note, because most people miss it. They say Adam and Eve's *pride* led to the fall. But I say it was their *doubt*, which led to fear, poor judgement and sin. I suggest that they never would have fallen for Satan's deception, had they not first *doubted God's word*. Think about it. Didn't Satan first *question* God's word? Didn't he twist that word to stir up insecurity, confusion and distrust? (Look at Genesis 3:1-5)

---

[8] Genesis 3:4-5

Of course he did! And he tries to do the same thing to me and you today. He knows that <u>doubt toward God's word opens the door to destruction</u>.

What did doubt do for the first family? It got them kicked out of the garden and cursed with suffering, toil and death.[9] Why didn't God just forgive them? Because He couldn't. His perfect justice demanded punishment. (To forgive their sin would have been to *condone* it, something a true and holy God cannot do.)

As a result, the Shalom peace of the garden was replaced by a world of strife and Satanic oppression. The fallen "human condition" became dominated by death, rebellion, perversion and seperation from God.

FALLEN FAMILY TRAITS

Is it any wonder, then, that we come from "dys-functional" families plagued by addictions, obsessions, divorces, abuses, etc.? No. It's no wonder, because we all have the same polluted bloodline. We share the same hereditary disease of sin. And we inherit the same fallen family traits, as a result. Here are some you should under-stand.

GUILT: It came as the immediate consequence of sin. After eating the fruit, Adam and Eve's eyes were opened to good and evil, and they became aware of their guilt before God. And the same disturbing awareness troubles people today.

This inborn sense of guilt has been exploited by some in the church, over the years, and by others who seek

---

[9] Genesis 3:16-19

to manipulate and control others through "guilt trips." (Ever met such people?) We're quick to judge others, too, because of our preoccupation with guilt. We're even prone to self-condemnation.

SHAME: Before the fall, Adam and Eve were *God*-centered, *other*-centered and totally unashamed. They were open. But after the fall, everything changed. They became *self-absorbed*. Their "self-awareness" skyrocketed, while their "self-esteem" plummeted. They covered their nakedness in shame.

Now think about our self-esteem problems today. Are they connected to sin? You better believe it. That's why education can't cure them, science can't solve them and psychology can't change them. Shame remains an inbred part of our fallen condition.

FEAR: After the fall, Adam hid from God, then explained, "*I was afraid because I was naked.*"[10]   Fear has been our dominant motivator, ever since the fall. One fear, of course, is our fear of God. But this isn't the biblical "fear of the Lord," that is healthy and positive. This is plain 'ol hide-in-the-bushes fear! We hide from God – sometimes behind religious masks and rituals, sometimes in total rebellion – because we don't like being naked before Him. Or we run away because we possess a false and frightening impression of Him.

Then there's our fear of death. The mere thought of it terrorizes us! How do we deal with death? Most of us deny the whole subject. We refuse to discuss it and we try to ignore it by keeping it out of sight in hospitals, convalescent homes and mortuaries.

---

[10] Genesis 3:10

We turn away from death because it reminds us of our own mortality, and our need to deal with eternal issues – like God. We attempt to suppress our fear of death by obsessing on drugs, drinking, sports, sex, entertainment, travel, business or other escapist pursuits. We try to lose ourselves in hero-worship and larger-than-life causes, too. Some people even try to escape their fear of death by *obsessing on death*! But no matter how we try to deny it, death is on the doorstep, haunting each and every person.

Fear makes slaves of us, as well. For instance, we fear rejection, so we become slaves to approval. We fear mediocrity, so we become slaves to status. We fear poverty, so we become slaves to "security." We fear weakness, so we chase after power. Yes, we're dominated by fear, and driven to extreme measures to tame it.

SELF-RIGHTEOUSNESS: We naturally point fingers, look for scapegoats and avoid accountability. Adam blamed Eve. Eve blamed the serpent.[11] And the beat goes on and on. (Just ask the kids who broke the vase!) Dishonesty and hypocrisy are made of this stuff.

OPPRESSION: After the fall, men became rulers over women,[12] and the strong of both sexes became dominators of the weak, physically, politically and economically. Such domination naturally breeds arrogance and cruelty in the oppressor, and *resentment* in the oppressed. You know how this works if you've ever had to endure an oppressive boss, parent, spouse or teacher. In turn, resentment breeds revolution, which explains why our globe is constantly embroiled in it.

---

[11] Genesis 3:12-13
[12] Genesis 3:14-16

STRIFE: We're competitive, or jealous, too, just as Adam and Eve's sons, Cain and Abel, were.[13]   Cain and Abel pioneered the art of "sibling rivalry." That rivalry, like most competition, was fueled by their insecurity about being "overlooked," "left behind" or "second best." Like most competition, it left them divided, alienated and ultimately defeated. (Think how many "losers" stand behind every sports champion.) Whereas *cooperation* marked human relations before the fall, competition has been the "natural" state of humanity ever since.

VIOLENCE: Cain murdered Abel. He did so because he felt the pain of "losing," and surrendered to the Satanic power that came with it.[14] This began the vicious cycle of hatred and violence that poisons individuals, groups and nations today. It takes the form of "eye for an eye" retribution or gang-style "revenge." It can surface in "crimes of passion," outbursts of anger, or even in abusive words. It's the former victim who victimizes, or the pain-filled person who lashes out at others. But no matter how you slice it, people hurt people – every day, in every way.

OUTSIDE THE KINGDOM

The painful truth is this. 100% of us were born in bondage to sin, fear, guilt, shame and death. We are sinners born outside the gates of God's kingdom, in the darkness of Satan's domain. We were born into Adam's fallen family.

---

[13] Genesis 4:1-24
[14] Genesis 4:7

Thank God we don't have to stay there.

CHAPTER TWO

The Prince of Peace

"For God rescued us from the power of darkness,
and brought us safe into the kingdom of
His dear Son." – Colossians 1:13

Yes, God has given us a way out. His name is Jesus. The liberator of captives, the conqueror of death, the Son of God, the Prince of Peace. He's the Lamb of God who takes away the sin of the world![1]

When I finally saw Jesus for who He is in all His goodness and glory, I instantly recognized my true condition. The vanity of my pursuits, the emptiness of my life and the sinfulness of my heart were instantly exposed. I was stripped naked and could no longer deny my weakness, poverty or bondage. I saw that I was a slave to sin and was doomed to die.

But in the same instant, I saw Jesus radiating all the things I lacked and desperately needed. Purity. Peace. Freedom. Forgiveness. Eternal life. And love. Total and unconditional. All embracing. Irresistible love.

He didn't just radiate these things, either. He offered them, saying, "Here, I've come so you could have these

---

[1] John 1:29

things. Please receive them. Take them as your own, then come, follow Me."

Who is this incredible Prince? What has He done for us? Where does He lead us? To live as children of God, we need some answers.

OUR RESCUE

"Anyone who sins is the slave of sin," said Jesus, "(but) if the Son sets you free, you will be free indeed."[2] The apostle Paul wrote, "It was for freedom that Christ set us free."[3]

Last chapter we talked about Adam's fall. We looked at our slavery to sin and death and a bunch of other bad news. But now let's look at the good news of our liberation. How did Jesus Christ set us free?

He acted as our kinsman redeemer.

What's a kinsman redeemer? To understand, we must go to the Old Testament book of Ruth. There we meet Naomi, a poor and hopeless widow, who returns from a foreign country to her home town of Bethlehem. She's lost everything. Her husband and sons have died, and only one of her foreign daughters-in-law, Ruth, has stayed with her. Naomi is a charity case. She and Ruth live off of barley trimmings left in the fields for the poor. Her family's ancestral land is long gone. Her status in the community is a thing of the past. She's down and out.

This is where a kinsman redeemer comes into the picture. By Jewish law, the closest male relative was ex-

---

2 John 8:34-36
3 Galatians 5:1

pected to redeem, or rescue, his distressed relatives, whenever possible. Such relatives usually became enslaved or destitute due to debt or distaster. But whatever the reason, if someone fell into bondage or poverty, a kinsman redeemer became their hope.

By Jewish law, the redeemer had to be related to the distressed, and also had to be *willing* and *able* to pay for the relative's debt, to buy back freedom or lost land. In the story of Ruth, Naomi's eventual redeemer was Boaz, a single and wealthy relative. Boaz's compassion for Naomi moved him to act on her behalf by purchasing her family's lost property. By doing this, he restored her dignity in the community, and renewed her hope. As Naomi's kinsman redeemer, *Boaz was willing and able to do for her what she could not do for herself.* He rescued her from her miserable condition.

What does Boaz have to do with Jesus and you? If you think about it a minute, the connection becomes clear. As we know, our natural family fell into bondage to sin, fear and death. This was the penalty, or debt, of Adam and Eve's offense against God. Spiritual poverty and lost dignity were suffered by all people, as a result. And because every person born since Adam has become part of the same bankrupt family, there's never been anyone capable of redeeming the human race.

Only Jesus could act as our kinsman redeemer. But this required a couple of things.

First, it required that God's creative Spirit take on human flesh, so as to be "related" to the rest of humanity, since only a relative could be a kinsman redeemer. In the physical person of Jesus, God did this. He proved Himself *willing* to redeem us. Second, it required a *virgin born* person, because only someone conceived outside of man's corrupt bloodline would be free from bondage and poverty. So Jesus was supernaturally born of a virgin.Like Adam, Jesus of Nazareth started life with a "clean slate." He was sinless. But unlike Adam, He *resisted* temptation.[4] He did not doubt or disobey. Therefore, He was *able* to "pay the price" of redemption, because He was rich in righteousness. Paul explained,

> "You know the grace of our Lord Jesus
> Christ, that though He was rich, He became
> poor for your sake, that through His poverty
> you might become rich."[5]

Jesus was perfectly innocent and unstained by sin. He was free from the power of death. Yet He was *willing* to take your death sentence upon Himself. His love compelled Him to meet you in your distress, then trade places! Hence, your sins were forgiven and your record cleared. You were liberated not by anything *you* did, but by what Jesus did for you as your kinsman redeemer. He paid the total price of your freedom – death.

Please understand this. It's why every religion on earth is inferior to the work of Christ. You see, religious systems always tell YOU how to become "good," or approved by God. Hindus tell you to meditate and control yourself. Moslems tell you to bow toward Mecca five times a day. Mormons tell you to earn merit through various

---

[4] Luke 4:1-13
[5] II Corinthians 8:9

works. In other words, they tell you your salvation is up to you! They load you down with burdens. They set you up with false hopes. They shackle you in religious bondage. But they never set you free from sin and death. They can't! The Bible says,

> "For it is by grace you have been saved, through faith – and this not from yourselves, it is the gift of God – not by works, so that noone can boast."[6]

Jesus did all the work. He paid the total price, as a gift. His death on the cross satisfied God's perfect justice. He suffered the penalty of sin for everyone. He delivered the ultimate pardon, and set the captives free! The apostle Paul explained it all this way,

> "So then, as the one sin (of Adam) condemned all men (to death), in the same way the right-eous act (of Jesus) sets all men free and gives them life."[7]

Can you believe this incredible truth? Yes, Jesus was the perfect kinsman redeemer. Like Boaz in the story of Ruth, He was related, compassionate and "wealthy" enough to purchase your freedom. He rescued you from the shackles of sin, shame, guilt, fear and death. He paid off all your debts and set you free – along with the whole fallen family!

---

[6] Ephesians 2:8
[7] Romans 5:18

HIS KINGDOM

So why do we still struggle with fallen family traits and old patterns of sin? Why don't we feel, or truly *experience,* the freedom Christ purchased for us? Why isn't liberation an everyday *reality* for most Christians? The answer comes on the other side of the cross.

As Christians, we tend to emphasize the death of Christ and almost ignore His resurrection (except on Easter). We focus on His forgiveness of our sins, not on the new life He gives us. Hence, the cross is Christianity's symbol, and not the empty tomb. But is that right? Isn't the cross only half the story? Yes, we must move beyond the cross to see the whole picture. True freedom awaits us – in the kingdom of God.

To understand this, it's helpful to look at slavery in the United States, where, after the Civil War, all slaves were set free. They were made le*gally* free. But think about it. Were they made *practically* free, or "free indeed?" No, not really. Why not? Because they weren't given the power or resources of freedom. The old oppression and racism, and the old economic structures didn't go away. The former slaves didn't receive a *new order of life* to match their legal freedoms.

Without this new order of life, they were doomed to further bondage. Many "freemen" fell back into poverty, or legal slavery. The cards of the world were stacked against the former slaves, and they still are. This remains the shameful legacy of political liberty without social or economic transformation. Without real power and a new order, freedom doesn't work.

This is why Jesus Christ brought you much more than freedom alone.

As the fully human Son of Man, Jesus acted as your kinsman redeemer, and paid your penalty. His death set you free. But as the fully divine Son of God, He ushered in a new order of existence. He introduced a *heavenly realm of transforming power* – the kingdom of God. And He invites you to enjoy its resources *today*, not just when you die!

What is the kingdom of God?

I had no idea for the first several years of my Christian life. Noone seemed to know about it, care about it or talk about it. So I didn't realize <u>the kingdom of God was the central theme of Jesus' ministry</u>. But it's true!

Jesus was passionate about establishing the new order of God's kingdom. It was His mission and purpose.[8] He taught about the kingdom and He told parables about the kingdom. He instructed followers to pray for the kingdom, to seek first the kingdom and to represent the kingdom. His actions demonstrated the kingdom. Hence, to not understand the kingdom is to miss Jesus entirely!

So what <u>is</u> the kingdom of God? Different people have different opinions. This is true because Jesus left the kingdom something of a mystery. He taught that the kingdom is something to enter,[9] and yet it's something to *inherit*.[10] The kingdom is both a *present* reality,[11] and a

---

[8] Luke 4:43
[9] Matthew 7:21
[10] Matthew 25;34
[11] Luke 17:20

future promise.[12] It's both a personal *experience*,[13] and a cataclysmic *event*.[14] In other words, it's something scholars will debate about till the cows come home!

But leave it to the apostle Paul to get to the point. He states simply, "The kingdom of God is not a matter of words, but of power."[15] Yes, power. Not political or social, or even economic power, but something far greater. He's talking about *the power of God*, which is spiritual and liberating. "Where the Spirit of the Lord is," Paul wrote, "there is liberty."[16]

Jesus embodied the kingdom. His acts demonstrated it's liberating and restoring power. He healed the sick. He cast out demons. He raised the dead. He forgave sins. He brought God's presence "down to earth" where people could grasp it. He invaded Satan's "turf" and showed His superiority. His kingdom clearly defeated demonic strongholds and overcame the effects of sin.

We can summarize by saying <u>the kingdom of God is the presence and power of God's Spirit, which liberates us from the dominion of sin and Satan</u>. It came first in Jesus, then more widely at Pentecost, when the Holy Spirit was made available to all who received Christ.[17]

It's this realm of God's Spirit that provides a "new order" of life in which we can maintain our liberty. And in this fallen world, that's some pretty awesome power!

---

[12] Matthew 8:11

[13] Romans 14:17

[14] Matthew 25:31

[15] I corinthians 4:20

[16] II Corinthians 3:17

[17] Acts 1:8-2:47

This power restores the pre-fall conditions Adam and Eve enjoyed in the garden, which we discussed last chapter. Remember the abundant life they enjoyed in harmony with God and with each other? Remember the unity and peace of "heaven on earth?" Now compare that picture of life with Paul's statement, "the kingdom of God is righteousness, peace and joy in the Holy Spirit."[18] Sounds pretty close, doesn't it?

And how about the "fruits of the Spirit?" Love, joy, peace patience, kindness, goodness, faithfulness, gentleness and self-control.[19] Don't they sound like they're fresh from the garden? And just read the second chapter of Acts to see how Pentacost ushered in a new and supernatural style of life among Christians. A lifestyle of sharing and caring that was out of this world! This was the wholeness of life, or Shalom, that Jesus came to give us through His resurrection and the power of the Holy Spirit. It's called "kingdom life."

I want to testify to this life because, as I mentioned in the introduction, I struggled as a Christian for some time. I knew in my mind I was forgiven and free, but I wasn't really *experiencing* it. The "kingdom of God" was just religious jargon. Empty words. But then, by God's grace, I discovered the kingdom, and yielded myself to it. I *experienced* "righteousness, peace and joy in the Holy Spirit." I entered the new order of God's kingdom and finally experienced resurrection power and freedom. And so can you.

---

[18] Romans 14:17
[19] Galatians 5:22-23

ENTERING THE KINGDOM

How do you enter the kingdom? By saying "yes" to God's invitation. By faith.

You enter by believing the truth. Yes, the kingdom of God exists. Jesus established it here on earth, then sent the Holy Spirit to expand it. It's the realm of God's liberating presence and power, and Jesus invites you to dwell in it. Do you believe it? Will you enter it?

So much depends on your response to God's word. If you doubt the kingdom exists, you won't enter it or enjoy its benefits. Oh sure, you might be "legally" free in Christ, but you'll *practically* struggle with fallen family traits and old patterns of sin. You'll labor in the poverty and bondage of the world's oppressive order. Your doubt will keep you in chains.

But if you'll enter the kingdom of God by faith, you'll experience the "peace that surpasses all understanding."[20] You'll enjoy the presence and power of God, which drives out bitterness, anger, insecurity, or anything else that's holding you back. It's true. God's word says the kingdom consists of righteousness, peace and joy in the Holy Spirit. You can believe this is the truth, and bet your life on it.

But you must decide where you wish to live. In God's kingdom or in the world. Under His loving rule or under Satan's control. In freedom or in sin.

Jesus calls you to enter the "narrow gate" leading to life, instead of the popular "wide gate" that leads to destruc-

---

[20] Philippians 4:7

tion.[21] He wants you to discard your worldly baggage and "come clean" into the kingdom. This is what "repent" means, to reject the old in favor of the new, to abandon the world in favor of the kingdom.

"Repent," said Jesus, "for the kingdom of God is at hand."[22]

When I stood at the kingdom gate, I trembled in fear. I was obsessed with what I had to "give up" and leave behind, because I didn't know what lay ahead. I didn't understand the treasure of God's kingdom, or the abundant life it offers. But I took a step of faith anyway, and am glad I did.

How about you? Have you entered the kingdom? Here's a prayer.

> Thank you, Lord Jesus, for setting me free.
> Thank you for paying the price of my liber-
> ation on the cross. Thank you for your incred-
> ible love! I say "no" to the sin and death of this
> fallen world and "yes" to resurrection life in
> your kingdom. I say "yes" to entering through
> the narrow gate and "yes" to your invitation
> – by faith! Amen.

---

[21] Matthew 7:13-14
[22] Mark 1:15

CHAPTER THREE

The Royal Adoption

"In love, God predestined us to adoption through
Jesus Christ to Himself." – Ephesians 1:5

When you entered God's kingdom, you became a
very special person. How special? Just listen to Jesus.

"I tell you the truth," He said. "Among those
born of women there has not risen anyone
greater than John the Baptist. Yet he who
is least in the kingdom of heaven is greater
than he."[1]

A pretty incredible statement, isn't it?! After all,
John the Baptist was Jesus' earthly cousin. He was miraculously conceived, and specially anointed to minister "in the
spirit and power of Elijah."[2] He came before Jesus, preaching repentance and salvation, preparing the way of the Lord.
He was probably the purest, most zealous servant of God to
ever come down the pike!

And yet, according to Jesus, John the Baptist couldn't
hold a candle to you or me in the kingdom.

---

[1] Matthew 11:11
[2] Luke 1:11-17

How can this be so? It's pretty simple, actually. You see, as great as John the Baptist was, he still lived under the old order. He came before the kingdom was established by Jesus or expanded by the Holy Spirit at Pentecost. <u>He was a *servant* of God, but not a child of God</u>.   He never got to enjoy the Spirit of adoption.

THE SPIRIT OF ADOPTION

Last chapter we talked about entering the kingdom, or realm of God's Spirit.   Now we must understand that in the kingdom, *God's Spirit enters us, as well*. The apostle Paul wrote to Christians, "Don't you know that you are a temple of God, and that the Spirit of God dwells in you?"[3] That same Spirit turns each of us into utterly new people. We become citizens of God's kingdom, with new rights, responsibilities and loyalties. And we become members of the Royal Family, as adopted children of God.

These radical changes result from the ministry of the Holy Spirit, which Paul called the Spirit of adoption.[4] He used the language of "adoption," even though it was a foreign term (Roman, not Jewish), to express a dramatic change of identity that is rarely understood today.

This dramatic change can be seen in Paul, himself, who, before meeting Christ, was known as Saul. Saul was a zealous Jew, a highly educated lawyer and "upwardly mobile" religous leader. He had all the credentials, he even came from a "good family." Saul's only problem was he was killing Christians!

---

[3] I Corinthians 3:16
[4] Romans 8:15, 23, 29, Galatians 4:5

Everything changed when Saul encountered the risen Lord – even his name. Saul became known as Paul, a new creature, citizen of the kingdom and ambassador for Christ. He regarded his old identity and credentials as "rubbish."[5] His transformation was total.

Today this same transformation leads Christians all around the world to take new names as an outward expression of their spiritual adoption. For instance, Mother Teresa, the Nobel prize winner from Calcutta, was born Ganxhe Agnes Bojaxhiu. She changed her name to Sister Mary Teresa of the Child Jesus, years ago, as a sign of her citizenship in God's kingdom.

Paul was inspired to use "adoption" to convey the radical nature of true conversion. Being a lawyer, he understood that adoption meant the official termination, or "death," of a person's old identity, for the sake of a new life with a new family. Just like today, adoption meant a new name, a new family and new relationships all around. So Paul, once the bitter enemy of God's children, became an adopted child of God. He then assured his Christian brothers and sisters,

> "The Spirit Himself bears witness with our
> spirit that we are children of God, and if
> children, heirs also, heirs of God and fellow
> heirs with Christ."[6]

This is earth-shaking, mind-blowing, life-changing stuff, don't you think?! The Bible says that Jesus, the one

---

[5] Philippians 3:7-11
[6] Romans 8:16-17

and only Son of God, THE Crown Prince of all creation, is
not ashamed to call you His brother or sister.[7] It says that
you are part of <u>a new race of people</u>, destined to be like
Him![8] As a citizen of the kingdom, you're not only adopted,
you're a royal prince or princess!

A POSITIVE SELF-IMAGE

This has affected me deeply because, before I em-
braced my adoption, my identity was based on credentials
and appearances. I puffed myself up, boasting in my status
as an Ivy League college graduate, pro football player,
business owner, even Mercedes-Benz driver. I gloried in
my physical strength. I was proud of owning a home in an
exclusive area. I was determined to build a positive self-
image.

But now, like Paul, I consider these things rubbish
compared to being a child of God. And whatever labels the
world might want to give me, I refuse to define myself by
them.   Even in the church, I refuse to be defined by
secondary factors such as my role, my gifting, my success or
failure. I can't allow my sense of identity or self-worth to
depend upon such outward and changeable things. I want
my self-esteem to stand rock solid on God's honest truth:
I'm a prince in His kingdom!

Now remember, the Spirit of God dwelling in us
testifies – and *confirms* – that this is the truth. We don't have
to huff and puff, or manufacture emotions. We need only
OPEN ourselves to the Holy Spirit, who fills us with

---

[7] Hebrews 2:11, Romans 8:29 and Matthew 12:50
[8] Romans 8:29

assurance and true self-esteem. Go ahead and let it happen right now where you're at. Let God confirm that <u>you are a prince or princess.</u> It's the truth, so you might as well accept it.

This is the ultimate "positive self-image." And believe me, self-image is important! For instance, if you think you're "ugly" or "stupid" or "worthless," you'll usually wind up living an ugly, stupid or worthless life. And even if you have a "successful" self-image in worldly terms, it won't necessarily produce a God-honoring life. This is why you must get your self-image straight.

Your true self-image, "child of God," comes from receiving Jesus and entering His kingdom, by faith. It's documented in the Word of God, and it's confirmed by the Holy Spirit. If you will embrace it, it can produce the most valuable, God-honoring life in the universe – a Christlike life.

THE "HALO EFFECT"

To further illustrate how special you are in God's kingdom, let me share what I know about the "halo effect." It began when God called my attention to John F. Kennedy Jr., the most special person I've ever known.

John and I got to know each other in a small class at Brown University, where we were both students. And even though I was the football star and upperclassman, he impressed the heck out of me.

There was a royal aura around him that turned heads everywhere he went, leaving people pointing and whispering, "Psst, that's John Kennedy Jr.!"

There was a special grace about him, too, a knowledge and confidence that was both casual and powerful, regal yet humble. He'd put you at ease, and yet make your heart rev faster than usual, just because you were near "Kennedy." Much more than any rich or famous people I'd ever met, John-John was *special*.

But as I thought about him in retrospect, I realized there was nothing special about *him* at all. Sure, he was a good guy, a fair athlete, a decent thinker. But so were thousands of other guys. No, the thing that put him on magazine covers and in the international spotlight, and the thing that gave him such presence, was *who he belonged to and what he represented*.

I realized that John F. Kennedy Jr. is special because he's RELATED to greatness. There's nothing he has done or could do to "earn" such special status. It was simply the result of the "halo effect."

What is the "halo effect?" It happens when <u>you gain self-esteem or special status by your proximity to greatness.</u> It operates if you're in the same restaurant as Bob Hope or Michael Jordan, if you go to the same hairdresser as Liz Taylor or Whitney Houston, or if you're related to someone famous. Whatever the case, you somehow "borrow" someone else's greatness, or "halo," and wear it as your own, usually for all it's worth! (Ever hear someone brag about their *uncle's neighbor's friend* who once rode the elevator with Elvis?!)

Do you see how the "halo effect" applies to you? You're special because <u>you belong to the living God</u>. <u>You represent the most powerful family of all</u>. <u>You're RELATED to Jesus, through the Spirit of adoption</u>!

Noone should enjoy a greater "halo effect" than you. Your "halo" is a royal crown, created and confirmed by the Holy Spirit. You're "aura" is that of a noble prince or princess. Your confidence is complete in Christ Jesus. As you walk in the love and grace of God, heads should turn and people should say, "Psst. That's a child of God!"

Now before you go to the next chapter, take a few minutes to let this all sink in. Open yourself to the Spirit of adoption, who testifies to the truth of your identity. Browse this chapter again, and consider what a REALLY positive self-image might do for you. Then take a moment to pray.

> Thank you, Lord Jesus, for leading me into
> your kingdom and into your family. Thank
> you for sending the Holy Spirit to confirm
> the truth of my adoption – the truth of my
> identity. Thank you for making me a
> new person – a royal prince or princess!
> Please help me to live as one. Amen.

CHAPTER FOUR

The Father King

"God has sent forth the Spirit of His Son into our hearts, crying, 'Abba! Father!'" – Galatians 4:6

I couldn't believe my ears. For the second time in a week, I was praying with a friend who addressed God as "Dad." And for the second time in a week, I was too shocked to say anything! But my mind raced with silent protests and questions.

Was this some kind of fad? It sounded like heresy, if not blasphemy. Who did they think they were, speaking to God so casually?!!

But as I mulled it over, I came to realize that God was using two very different people, one from South Africa and the other from Colorado, two people who had never met, to introduce me to something very important.

I could reach no other conclusion, because these friends were the most humble, gifted and Christlike people I knew. People of the word and of prayer. People who lived simply and gave freely. People whose lives were full of unmistakable and very frequent miracles.

What important thing were they introducing me to? The incredible reality of God as my intimate and heavenly Father. A life-changing reality I soon began to experience for myself, and a reality that Satan will fight like hell to keep YOU from experiencing because it's so important.

So beware of his efforts to distract or condemn you as you read this chapter. Beware of his efforts to build objections in your mind against this truth. More than anything, *be assured,*

"The Father Himself loves you," said Jesus, "because you have loved me and have believed that I came from the Father."[1]

Who is "the Father?" He's the one "who so loved the world that He sent His only begotten Son to save it."[2] He's the One who has blessed you with every spiritual blessing in Christ...the one who chose you before the foundation of the world...and predestined you to adoption, according to the kind intention of His will. <u>He's the one who grants you direct access to Himself through the Spirit, as a citizen of His kingdom and member of His household.</u>[3] In short, He's the one who sent Jesus to bring you into relationship with Himself.

Are you confused about the "Trinity" of Father, Son and Holy Spirit? If so, you don't have to be.

"Trinity" isn't a word found in scripture, it's simply the term used to describe the reality of God revealed in the Bible as "Father, Son and Holy Spirit." Does this mean there are three different Gods? No. We're talking about <u>one God</u> who is expressed three ways – way beyond our comprehension!

---

[1] John 16:27
[2] John 3:16
[3] Ephesians 1:3-6, 2:18-19

Now a God beyond comprehension upsets some people who want everything to come in neat packages, but unfortunately the Creator of the universe won't fit!

An early church theologian, named Augustine, tried to help us, anyway, by comparing God to a tree consisting of roots, trunk and branches. Each part, he said, is equally and essentially "tree," yet each has its own appearance and function. The Father, Son and Holy Spirit are, likewise, equally and essentially "God." Only their functions differ. The Holy Spirit (like branches), connects us to Jesus (the trunk), who then brings us to the Father (the root source of life). Does that help? I hope so.

THE UPSETTING ONE

However you explain it though, emotions run deep on the subject of God the Father, because fatherhood is a *painful* subject for many of us. This is true because we've been disappointed, if not deeply hurt, by fathers who failed us in some way.

We've been dominated, rejected, molested, abandoned, abused or ignored by our fathers. We've been pressured toward perfection or passively left unsupported, harshly treated or leniently indulged. In any case, most of us have lacked the balance of <u>*loving correction and positive affirmation*</u> that a father is supposed to provide.

Without this balanced fathering, we can easily grow rebellious toward authority and unsure of our identity and self-worth. Prostitutes and street kids are extreme examples of this. We can also lack a sense of belonging. Hence, today's gangs are filled with fatherless boys.

On the other hand, we can become overly *compliant* to authority, and wind up identifying ourselves by the institutions we "belong" to, such as colleges, clubs, political parties, companies, countries and even church denominations.

The point is, when we lack healthy fathering, we cry out for love, approval and a sense of belonging, and often wind up looking for them in the wrong places. Fortunately, we can STOP LOOKING when we find our heavenly Father.

Belonging to God the Father is *controversial,* however. It was for Jesus, and it will be for you, too. Jesus made waves by referring to God as "My Father."[4] He also called God, "Abba," which, in the local language meant "Daddy" or "Papa." This intimate and exclusive language outraged Jewish religious leaders who wanted to stone Him to death because "He was making Himself equal with God."[5]

Why did the religious leaders react so violently? One reason is that their leadership status was threatened by this radical and popular figure from Nazareth. They were like insecure bureaucrats who feared losing their power. He was exposing their hypocrisy and criticizing how they represented God.

But in all fairness, the Jewish leaders had some legitimate concerns about how people addressed God. For centuries they had carefully avoided direct references to God, or "Yahweh," out of sheer reverence and respect. They

---

[4] Luke 2:49, John 2:16, 5:17, etc.
[5] John 5:17

worshipped a *holy* God who delivered their nation from bondage in Egypt, and who gave them the Ten Commandments, the Promised Land and the prophets. This was an *awesome,* sovereign God, who was called a "father" only 15 times in the entire Old Testament. And if God *did* have a "son," they figured it was the nation of *Israel*, not Jesus! So Jesus' words struck a nerve for good reason.

His reference to God as "Abba, Father" was no gimmick, or senseless irritation, however. It was of the highest importance because, while the kingdom of God was the central theme of His *ministry*, the fatherhood of God was the focal point of Jesus' personality. <u>His identity and purpose flowed from His relationship with the Father.</u>

As a boy on a family trip, Jesus lingered behind at "His Father's house," the temple in Jerusalem.[6] As a dying man on the cross, Jesus took His last breath and committed His spirit to the Father.[7] In between, He said He was "sent" by the Father,[8] to bring honor to the Father.[9] He claimed exclusive knowledge of the Father,[10] extraordinary guidance from the Father,[11] and the full authority of the Father.[12] He said that to accept or reject Him, was to accept or reject the Father,[13] and insisted that He was the only way to the Father.[14]

---

[6] Luke 2:49
[7] Luke 23:46
[8] John 5:23, 37
[9] John 8:49
[10] John 10:15
[11] John 5:19-23
[12] John 5:22, 26-30
[13] Luke 10:16
[14] John 14:6

You can hear several of these themes in Jesus' classic statement,

> "All things have been handed over to me by my Father; and no one knows the Son except the Father, nor does anyone know the Father except the Son, and anyone to whom the Son wishes to reveal Him."[15]

REVEALING THE FATHER

How did Jesus reveal the Father? Jesus revealed the Father *through Himself.* The Bible states that Jesus was the "radiance of God's glory," and the *exact representation* of His nature.[16] Jesus said that anyone who saw *Him* was truly seeing the Father.[17] In other words, Jesus was a "spittin' image" of the Father, because He shared the very *essence* of God.[18]

Jesus revealed the Father through His teaching, as well. He sought to correct a distorted picture of God that existed in the minds of many. What was this picture? (Hint: it's the same one many people hold today.)

This picture portrayed God as a distant and impersonal dictator and judge. A "formula" God who rewards only those who observe the law and follow every rule of tradition. A dominating God who cripples people with negative and controlling regulations, managed by "elite"

---

[15] Matthew 11:27
[16] Hebrews 1:3
[17] John 14:9
[18] Colossians 1:19

religious leaders. A harsh and demanding God who wants nothing more than sacrifice. In short, a God who offers nothing but bondage to the common people.

How did Jesus correct this picture? He taught about His Father. By doing so, He used an image loaded with authority. Among the Jews, a father ruled his family. Even adult sons would remain dependent upon their fathers. Absolute obedience to fathers was assumed and fully understood. Hence, Jesus' reference to God the Father called to mind God's total authority, and the need for complete obedience to Him. And yet, fatherly authority was NOT Jesus' primary emphasis.

Jesus taught that God is a loving and perfect Father.[19] A watchful Father who rewards good deeds done in secret.[20] A generous Father who knows our needs, and wants to meet them.[21] A trustworthy Father who responds to those who seek Him.[22] A Father who is close and interested in every aspect of our lives!

His teaching about the Father brought God "down-to-earth" and into every part of daily life. This corrected the popular view of a distant, impersonal God. His use of "Abba, Father" modeled a living, intimate *relationship* with God, instead of a life based on religious *ritual*.

Jesus' teaching about the Father is perhaps best illustrated in His parable of the Prodigal Son.[23] Here, Jesus told of a father who forgave a selfish and disrespectful son who had left the family and wasted his inheritance on life in

---

[19] Matthew 5:48
[20] Matthew 6:1-18
[21] Matthew 6:26-34
[22] Matthew 6:7-11
[23] Luke 15:11-32

the fast lane. When the son finally "hit the wall" and repented, the father didn't "rub his nose in it," or read him the "riot act." Amazingly, he welcomed him home with open arms! He even celebrated by throwing an expensive party, and by restoring full privilege and authority to the son.

The father rejoiced, according to Jesus, because he viewed the son as reborn from the dead. In this story, the father demonstrated forgiveness, grace and mercy, all attributes Jesus wished to reveal about His Father – God.

"ABBA" FOR ALL

The fatherhood of God is more than a helpful analogy or theological novelty for us to think about – it's a spiritual reality that Jesus invites us to experience for ourselves. "Do not call anyone on earth 'Father,'" He said, "for you have one Father, He who is in heaven."[24] He encouraged us to "dial direct" to the Father in prayer,[25] and taught His followers to confidently pray, "Abba, Father."[26] Most of all, He modeled a relationship with the Father *for us to imitate*.

Please stop right here and take this to heart. Understand that true "discipleship" is all about *imitation*, NOT education. A true disciple, like a modern-day apprentice, may follow his/her master and learn for a while, but the ultimate goal of a disciple is to live the same style, or "way" of life on his/her own. For this reason, early believers called

---

[24] Matthew 23:9
[25] John 16:26
[26] Luke 11:2, Matthew 6:9, see commentaries on "Our Father."

themselves "people of the way," and imitated Jesus' relationship with the Father. They knew Jesus had lived as a "child of God," and had called them to follow suit.

There is evidence in fact, that to address God intimately as "Abba, Father" was a cherished privilege among first century Christians. It gave them a powerful – and deeply spiritual – bond with Jesus and with each other. Paul referred to this privilege in Galatians 4:6 and again in Romans 8:15, when he wrote,

> "For you have not received a spirit of slavery...
> but a spirit of adoption as sons by which we cry
> out, 'Abba! Father!'"

So what happened to this heart cry among Christians? Why isn't the fatherhood of God emphasized in the church today? Good questions, especially when you consider the New Testament is loaded with 245 references to the Father.

Apostles Paul and Peter both used greetings like, "Grace to you and peace from *God our Father* and the Lord Jesus Christ." In II Corinthians 1:3, Paul wrote, "Blessed be the God and Father of our Lord Jesus Christ, the Father of mercies and the God of all comfort." And Jesus Himself said,

> "An hour is coming, and now is, when true
> worshipers shall worship the Father in spirit
> and truth; for such people the Father seeks
> to be His worshipers."[27]

---

[27] John 4:23

So why isn't our Christian focus upon the Father? The answer probably lies in church history, where the person and work of the Holy Spirit was ignored for centuries.

As we discussed last chapter, it's the Holy Spirit who testifies to our adoption, and to our membership in God's household. It's the Holy Spirit who makes us members of God's "chosen race" and "royal priesthood." It's the Holy Spirit who enables us to become "brothers and sisters" in Christ. And it's the Holy Spirit who puts Royal Family crowns on our heads!

It's also the Holy Spirit who extends the Father's unconditional love, acceptance and affirmation. This experience is best illustrated at Jesus' baptism. It was there that God touched Jesus through the Holy Spirit, and told Him, "You are my beloved Son, in you I am well pleased."[28] What a blessing of love and approval!

There's little doubt it created a deep sense of security in Jesus, which enabled Him to begin His ministry, resist temptation, and fulfill the Father's purpose for His life.

It's this same supernatural experience of love and acceptance that can bless us. It's the "love of God shed abroad in our hearts through the Holy Spirit"[29] that drives out fear and replaces it with kingdom confidence.

---

[28] Mark 1:11
[29] Romans 5:5

"ABBA" FOR ME

I can personally attest to the life-changing intensity of this experience. One Saturday morning several years ago, I encounted the Father's love quite by accident. It was at a time when a business of mine was at a critical crossroads that I decided to fast (i.e. not eat) for several days. I wanted to be sensitive to the Holy Spirit, in hopes of discerning God's will in the situation. I also wanted financial miracles and thought fasting might help!

Needless to say, my mind was *not* on the fatherhood of God – my mind was focused squarely upon money. In fact, I was sitting at our kitchen table that morning writing checks. As I did, I asked God a question. I was trying to determine how much money to give at church the next day. And because my financial future looked rather gloomy, I was not feeling charitable. I didn't feel very good about my pastor, either.

So as I sat struggling to decide on an amount, I asked God to help by giving me an exact figure, as I'd heard stories of Him doing that for other people. But no amount came to mind. God was silent. So, gritting my teeth, I asked whether the 10% "tithe" rule should be my guideline. But I didn't get an impression there, either. So, just as I concluded God didn't care about my petty situation, I heard His "still quiet voice."

As plain as day, He told me, "Give how much you *want* to give, John." Instantly I knew this was the Father. His advice was so simple and so wise, it was fatherly! It set me free, and yet it cut to my heart. It revealed my bad attitude, and prompted a change in it, all at once. God's love

for my pastor and church welled up in me, and I suddenly
wanted to give generously, much more than 10%! I was
elated to know God was so near. I was amazed that God was
so interested in me and my everyday affairs. And then it
happened.

Somehow in my mind's eye, I was taken to the large
farmhouse where the prodigal son returned to his father. I
was ushered to a door, which I knew the Father was behind.
Hesitantly, I opened the door and stepped into the room –
and into His awesome presence. I was instantly and completely overwhelmed. I can't say what the Father looked
like exactly, because His glory was too bright! But I can say
what the Father *felt* like. His radiance was warm and
enveloping. His love was breathtaking, and His acceptance
was absolutely beyond description!

I was floored – literally. Lying face down on my
kitchen floor, I cried like a baby, unable to contain the
emotions I was feeling, as wave after wave of the Holy Spirit
swept through me. From my innermost being I was crying
out, "Abba! Father!"

I couldn't believe the insight that came with these
feelings. I realized how totally mistaken I'd been about
God. I realized I didn't have to work or perform to earn His
approval. It was complete. Jesus had done it all! I only had
to receive it. I didn't have to strive or compete with other
Christians for God's love, either – there's plenty to go
around! I realized there was nothing to fear anymore. My
insecurity was gone and I've felt like His beloved, adopted
and very secure son, ever since.

Perhaps you've had a similar experience, and you're saying, "Amen!" If so, I praise God with you. But if you haven't, I realize you're probably wondering whether this experience is reserved for "super-spiritual" types, or for "freak" encounters only. Well, the answer is no.

The experience of our Father's love and approval is for *you*, not just for once-in-a-lifetime events, but for everyday life. The key is *OPENING UP to the Holy Spirit*, in prayer, in worship, and in everyday situations. The Holy Spirit responds by welling up the Father's unconditional love for you, and for others, and instantly changes your heart from selfishness to sacrifice. With this love comes deep security and trust, which prompts you to seek the Father's will, not your own. (See Jesus' incredible example in Mark 14:36).

I've experienced "the love of God shed abroad in my heart through the Holy Spirit" many times and in many ways. And it usually leads to *tears* being shed abroad on my face! You can't help but cry it seems, when the love of "Daddy" engulfs you.

I've had the joy of praying for and worshipping with other brothers and sisters who've felt the same thing, while experiencing the Father's blessing of love and approval. But once again, the key in most cases is an *openness to God's Spirit*. The Holy Spirit confirms your adoption, and affirms the Father's love for you. And this opens the floodgates to transformed kingdom living.

Husbands who experience the Father's love can love their wives and children in the same unconditional way. They can minister loving correction and guidance. Men who are secure in the Father's love can be vulnerable, gentle and compassionate. They can be liberated from insecurity-based "macho" roles, which produce emotional paralysis and pain.

Women who know the Father's love are also freed to love in new and healthier ways. They can confidently assert themselves to overcome oppression or prejudice, yet they can still nurture and support. They are motivated by love, not anger. Children who receive the Father's love through parents also enjoy new security and confidence. In other words, people who experience the Father's love can live abundant, kingdom lives.

Why aren't more Christians enjoying this new order of existence? There are three primary reasons.

1.)   The first is the commonly distorted view of God, as harsh judge or distant dictator. Such distortions often flow from bad experiences with natural fathers and from legalistic religion. In either case, Jesus' revelation of the Father is missed.

2.)   The second reason is the widespread ignorance and neglect of the Holy Spirit. This has been caused, in part, from the church's reaction against extremist or heretical Holy Spirit "movements" in history. But by not fully recognizing the Holy Spirit's role and personality, many Christians have missed the reality of adoption and intimacy with the Father.

This chapter has attempted to deal with these issues, hopefully with some success. But there is another reason Christians fail to experience the Father's blessing.

3.)   This third reason is the *holiness* of the Father. Jesus revealed the *perfect* Father. His love and grace is balanced by His *righteousness and truth.* Hence, He doesn't tolerate our sinful attitudes and behaviors. His presence exposes the sin in our lives. Therefore, a life of intimacy with the Father demands purity.

This causes us to do one of two things. Either we confess our sins and "come clean" through repentance and forgiveness, or we run the other way!

If we run, it's usually because we refuse to drop the baggage (pet hurts, idols, etc.) of our past, and are afraid to confess our need for change.

We see the fallen fathers who rejected us, abused us, neglected us, or abandoned us, rather than the One who rescued and adopted us. As a result, we refuse to let go of deeply rooted attitudes of rebellion, bitterness, fear, anger, judgment, and unforgiveness. We cling to our unbelief, denying that Jesus has shown us the unconditional love of the Father.

These attitudes then serve as barriers to intimacy with our "Abba, Father." We just can't seem to get close to Him.

BREAKING THROUGH THE "ABBA" BARRIER

To enjoy the wholeness and freedom that come from intimacy with the Father, these barriers must come down and we must be healed. This happens when we do two things.

First, <u>we must forgive the people who have sinned against us in our lives</u>. We must ask God to help reveal who they are, and how we should forgive them. He will answer, but be advised, this process can be painful because it exposes our worst hurts and disappointments over the years, and asks us to deal with them. It can cause us to confront long buried and easily denied anger, too, or other emotions that produced fear and isolation. It can even cause us to make apologies or restitution.

This is a deeply emotional process which is usually helped along by a trusted prayer partner, small group or counselor. But it's the only way to be healed and liberated from your past, so you can embrace your future. It's the only way to discard your former, dysfunctional family patterns, in favor of God's functional, Royal Family pattern. It's the *only way* to live like a child of God.

Forgiveness is so important, Jesus told us to forgive up to *490 times*, if need be![30] He also told us,

> "If you forgive people when they sin against you, your heavenly Father will also forgive you. But if you don't forgive others, your Father will not forgive you."[31]

---

[30] Matthew 18:21,22
[31] Matthew 6:14-15

Yes, forgiveness is central to living with the Father, as a child of God – as evidenced by Jesus, who forgave even the people who mocked and killed Him.[32]

Next, <u>we must repent of the bitter judgments, vows, habits and rebellious attitudes that reside in our hearts</u>. These can include judgments against God, whom we may blame for past sufferings or setbacks, as well as judgments against people. These attitudes are often deeply buried. But the Holy Spirit will expose them if we're willing to be open. And once exposed, we must confess them as sins and repent of them. By repent, I mean "turn away from," "reject" and utterly "renounce."

I recall the night my wife and I ministered to a HIV-infected Christian brother who had come out of homosexuality. He had entered that lifestyle in search of love, knowing it was wrong, yet propelled by the pain and confusion of his past. He had been molested by a neighbor when he was four years old, raped when he was twelve, and sexually assaulted by his father, at the age of fifteen.

Now he knew he was saved by Jesus, but was struggling to get close to the Father. He wanted a breakthrough of intimacy.

So we prayed together. As we did, we asked if he had forgiven his attackers and the other people who had hurt him, and he said "yes." But just to make sure, we led him through those prayers again, person by person. But there was no breakthrough.

We stayed in prayer, waiting on the Holy Spirit, when I heard the Father's voice whisper, "He hasn't for-

---

[32] Luke 23:34

given Me." I wasn't sure I'd heard correctly, so I kept waiting. But the same words kept coming up, so I finally asked our friend, "Have you forgiven God?"

He immediately broke into tears. No, he hadn't forgiven God, which meant he hadn't repented of *his judgment* against God for allowing people to hurt him.

Sin was separating him from the Father, the sin of judgement and bitterness. But as he confessed his sin and repented of it, he experienced the Father's love. Right there in our living room, he cried and cried, awash in the Father's love and forgiveness.

When I first opened myself to the Holy Spirit's ministry (through a trusted friend), He performed radical "heart surgery" which enabled me to know and obey the Father in a more intimate way. In the process, I had to work through the emotional process of repentance and forgiveness. It was painful and humbling, and there was more healing to follow. But it began to set me free, and release new joy into my life. I'm certain it was this step that prepared me for the major breakthrough I described earlier, as well.

THE IMPORTANT FATHER

Breaking through the "Abba barrier" is incredibly important. So important I think, that the very quality of your *life* depends on it. True *Christlikeness* is born from it. So take it slowly. Reread last section, if not the whole chapter, once or twice. Mull it over, meditate and let it sink into the very fiber of your soul. It's that important.

You may also want to ask God for a prayer partner, if you don't already have one. But whatever you do, please don't run away from your Father!

Look to Jesus, and receive the Father He has given you. The Father who wants you to enjoy affirmation and security, wholeness and health. The Father who gladly adopted you and gave you a royal crown of righteousness. Go ahead and pray to Him now.

> Abba Father, thank you for revealing yourself
> to me through Jesus, your Son. Thank you for
> loving me and inviting me to call you "Daddy."
> Help me to receive this incredible privilege,
> by faith. Help me to live as your child.
> In Jesus' name I pray. Amen.

CHAPTER FIVE

Child of Faith

"We walk by faith, not by sight." – II Corinthians 5:7

Life in God's kingdom is an *adventure* of faith. The Royal Family is a *family* of faith. God's kingdom is a *realm* of faith. As an adopted child of God, you're called to a *life* of faith, as suggested by the Old Testament prophet, Habakkuk, who proclaimed, "The righteous shall live by faith."[1]

Unfortunately, many of us "talk the talk" of faith, but fail to walk the walk. That's because the path of faith can be bumpy and difficult! It's a journey that usually includes many twists and turns, scrapes and bruises! (I recommend John Bunyan's classic faith tale, *Pilgrim's Progress*, if you haven't considered this journey.)

A life of faith often seems like a *crawl* of faith, and yet I know that each of us is called to this life.

I caught a fresh glimpse of how this life works recently, in a game I call the "Trust Daddy" game. I played it with my seven year-old daughter Christina, and here's how it works. She covers her eyes with her hands, while I give her verbal commands to direct her steps around the room or house. I say, "Take three big steps forward," and she takes those steps, then waits to hear further instructions. Turn right, turn left, take five steps backwards, etc.

---

[1] Habakkuk 2:4

The first time we tried it, I was amazed. My wish was her command. Her steps were bold, her turns were sharp and her confidence was sky high! After we had played awhile, she returned to me, now with her eyes open and a big smile on her face. I was joyfully praising her for demonstrating such faith in my words of direction.

And then I saw it. Something in her face changed. I couldn't bear to ask, but I had to. "Christina," I said, "were you peeking?" Slowly she nodded her head, affirming the worst. "Aaaah!" I howled in my heart. My own daughter couldn't even trust me to guide her around her room!

Needless to say, I've been trying to build up my "trust account" with her ever since, and I'm glad to report she now plays "Trust Daddy" without cheating!

The point I want to make is how strongly we yearn to "see where we're going." We want to "see for ourselves." We insist we'll, "believe it when we see it!"

In our visual world, we depend on our eyes. We want to see "facts" and "proof," before we step into anything. Because of deeply ingrained fear, we're very cautious and *distrustful toward what we can't see with our eyes.*

Unfortunately, we're often deceived by what we *do* see! Eve saw the attractive (and forbidden) fruit, and fell into sin.[2] Ten of Israel's twelve spies saw the "gigantic" tribes inhabiting the Promised Land and fell into fear, which cost them forty years in the wilderness.[3] Israel's army saw the giant warrior, Goliath, and fell into paralysis.[4] Jesus'

---

[2] Genesis 3:6
[3] Numbers 13-14
[4] I Samuel 17:11

disciples saw a storm and despite the miracles they'd already seen, fell into a panic.[5]   We too are suckers for what we see. And with today's multi-media illusions, high-tech special effects and visual marketing technology, our eyes don't stand a chance!

Kingdom life calls us to a different approach. We know that our Father is invisible, yet very present and active. Hence, we must walk by *faith*, which is defined as, "the assurance of things hoped for, *the conviction of things not seen*."[6]   We must remind ourselves that,

> "Without faith it is impossible to please God,
> for he (or she) who comes to God must believe
> that He is, and that He is a rewarder of those who
> seek Him."[7]

In other words, we must break our natural tendency to walk by sight alone. Now that we've broken through the "Abba Barrier," and learned that our Father is *for* us and *with* us in everything we do, we can break through the "faith barrier." How do we do this?

We affirm that "faith comes by hearing."[8] We remember that God communicates by the "word of the Lord," and that Jesus said, "Those who have ears to hear, let them hear."[9] So we open our ears and listen!

---

[5] Mark 4:35-40
[6] Hebrews 11:1
[7] Hebrews 11:6
[8] Romans 10:17
[9] Matthew 11:15

We listen for our Father's voice, knowing that as children of God, we're to be "led by the Spirit."[10]   We respond to God's word which says, "trust in the Lord with all your heart, and do not lean on your own understanding."[11] We trust that "Father knows best." <u>We look to Jesus, always seeking to imitate His radical dependence on the Father</u>.

And this isn't easy. It goes against all our worldly training, which has sought to make us *independent*. As we grow up in our earthly families, we're trained to do more *on our own*. Independence is expected and applauded. But in God's kingdom, everything's reversed. We're called to become more and more *dependent* upon God. As we mature in the Royal Family, we're supposed to do less on our own.

As in the "Trust Daddy" game I described above, we must believe our Father loves us and wants to carefully guide us around obstacles and into true freedom and wholeness. We must believe that God sees the whole picture, while our view is limited. We must believe He'll lead us along the path to abundant life, if we'll trust and obey His voice.

How does God guide us, once we believe these truths? There are four primary ways.

HIS SPIRIT

As Christians, we are truly "anointed ones," filled with the Holy Spirit. Jesus said concerning the Spirit,

---

[10] Romans 8:14 and Galatians 5:16
[11] Proverbs 3:5

"When He, the Spirit of truth comes, He will guide you into all truth, for He will not speak on His own initiative, but what He hears, He will speak."[12]

We've already discussed how the Holy Spirit offers us the experience of adoption and the loving reality of God as "Abba, Father." The Holy Spirit puts a Royal Family crown on our head which we receive by faith. Now picture that crown – equipped with earphones!

Yes, our Father guides us and speaks to us through the Holy Spirit who dwells in us. He can do this through dreams, visions, songs, literature, films or through sudden words of revelation. Such words can come to us when we hear preaching, when we receive ministry from brothers and sisters, or even when we talk with complete strangers! Sometimes this guidance is dramatic, when revelation just explodes into our consciousness, and other times it's very subtle, just a quiet nudge or confirmation.

A recent experience illustrates what I'm talking about. I was in an unfamiliar part of Los Angeles, tanking up my car with gas. As I drove down the onramp to rejoin the freeway, I spotted a hitchhiker. My first reaction was my normal reaction – to just pass by. I almost *never* pick up hitchhikers, especially in a strange parts of L.A. So I sped up to pass the man.

But as I did, I sensed God saying, "Stop and pick him up!" I tried to resist this word, but it was a *significant* nudge. Because I was being obedient that day, I hit the brakes and

---

[12] John 16:13

pulled over. The hitchhiker ran down the ramp to join me.

No sooner had he climbed into the car, then he spotted my Bible on the floor. Immediately he started spilling his guts about his life. He was a "backslidden" Christian reaping hard times and broken relationships because of the sin in his life. He understood his situation, too. All he needed was a touch from God, and he would be back on the right path.

Through our meeting and conversation, he got that touch, especially when we pulled off the freeway, parked and prayed together. Through the Holy Spirit, God ministered powerfully to this man. He received new revelation about his life and circumstances, loving affirmation about his place before God, and hope for his future. Our loving Father had led one son, via the Holy Spirit, to reach – and touch – another son.

There are many dramatic guidance stories I could share, but the more frequent type are of the quiet nudge variety. You know the type. Apologize to your wife or husband. Give to a needy brother or sister. Put aside work to play with the kids. Help a neighbor look for a lost dog. Give a kind word to an abrasive phone solicitor. Let someone into your lane of traffic. Confess sin, repent, forgive, etc.

Quiet nudge guidance especially affects me when I'm asked to preach. Often, after preparing my best message, which is usually a hermeneutic "masterpiece," I'm nudged by the Holy Spirit toward the Father's message, which is normally very simple, straightforward and profound! This means I have to rip up my notes and start over. And this can be a real battle.

Here again, the real issue is faith. Do I have faith enough to trust God's prompting more than my ability or training? Do I have faith enough to surrender control? Do I have faith enough to trust and obey? These are the core questions of living by faith.

HIS WORD (THE BIBLE)

"All scripture is inspired by God," wrote the apostle Paul, "and is profitable for teaching the truth, rebuking error, correcting faults and giving instruction for right living."[13] The author of Hebrews wrote,

> "The word of God is living and active and
> sharper than any two-edged sword, and
> piercing as far as the division of soul and
> spirit, of both joints and marrow, and able
> to judge the thoughts and intentions of the
> heart."[14]

A pretty scary statement, isn't it? No wonder people don't read their Bibles! Sure, Father will speak to us through scripture. But we won't always like what He says!

To hear and walk with God however, we must *open ourselves* to the scriptures. This means putting aside our ready-made and self-righteous interpretations, and submitting to God when we read the Bible. Yes, this process can strip us naked. But then the scriptures can clothe us in the truth. Yes, the scriptures will correct us. But God only corrects those He loves.[15]

---

[13] II Timothy 3:16
[14] Hebrews 4:12
[15] Hebrews 12:6

As I turn to God's word, I find that my daily steps are ordered and corrected by the Father, who speaks through scripture. I know that His Spirit actively guided the writers of the Bible, and that His Spirit *in me* calls special attention to "now" words that impact my life today and my plans for tomorrow. And as much as I hate to be corrected, I've learned to embrace God's assurance,

> "Turn to my correction and, behold, I will pour out my Spirit upon you. I will make my words known to you."[16]

It's not all "tough love" in the word of God, either. The scriptures affirm and encourage us too. They reveal the Father, and who we are in Christ. They inject us with supernatural peace, joy and love. They fill us with hope. Frequently they seem to leap off the page with powerful – and very personal – words of insight, confirmation or promise. These revelations can mean the difference between a luke-warm life of religion and a vibrant life of faith. So go ahead and ask your Father for guidance and revelation through the scriptures. You can believe He'll speak to you through the Bible, so read and listen.

---

[16] Proverbs 1:23

OUR CIRCUMSTANCES

This is where open and closed "doors" of opportunity, "divine appointments" and unusual "coincidences" come into play. There is no doubt God works through our circumstances, both good and bad. Our Father is continually refining, testing, and reinforcing our faith through circumstances.

This is a challenging way to "hear" God, however. We're frequently tempted to read God into every situation, or jump to unwarranted conclusions. Because this is true, let me suggest that circumstances should either confirm or be confirmed by other indicators from God. Circumstances alone are rarely enough, since "open doors" don't always come from Him. In fact open doors can be *trap* doors! Hence, we need much wisdom, discernment and caution. But when circumstances do line up with other guidance factors, they can really build our faith!

I'm reminded of an incident related to this book. God had inspired me to write *Royal Family*, and had confirmed its message through each of the ways we're discussing. But at one point I became extremely discouraged and intimidated by the task, and finally put it aside. There was a film script I wanted to write instead, so I started working on that.

But as I did, I sensed God telling me I was moving in the wrong direction. I tried to resist this nudging because I had visions of an Academy award-winning film scipt. I didn't want to go back to the book, so I suppressed His "nudges" until they finally drove me to open myself in prayer one memorable morning.

That morning I told Father that if He *really* didn't want me writing the script, He'd have to make it OBVIOUS. I was in no mood for interpreting nudges.

That entire day I spent whirring away at my computer, creating one great scene after another for the film script. It was really going well. My creative juices were flowing, my productivity was at an all-time high. At last dinnertime came, so I prepared to shut down. But just as I was about to hit the "save" button, the lights went off. The power in half the house went down. A fuse had blown, for the first time ever, and with no apparent reason.

Instantly I realized I hadn't saved *any* of that day's work, and that I'd lost it all! Every bit of my work was erased, gone, flushed down the micro-circuit sewer! In shock, I remembered my prayer, and didn't know whether to laugh or cry.

God had "answered" my prayer and "spoken" through my circumstances – in the OBVIOUS way I'd requested. Needless to say, I got back to writing this book, confident it was God's will!

God also tests our faith through circumstances. Anyone familiar with suffering knows this reality. The tragic loss of loved ones, the victimization of innocents, or life setbacks of any kind can raise serious questions concerning God.

"Would this happen if God really existed?" "If God does exist and *does* love me, then why would He let this happen?" "Why me?" "Why this?" "Why now?" Why, why, why?! Difficult circumstances often produce confusion, anger and doubt.

Not long ago I grappled with these issues of faith when my wife, Suzi, suffered two miscarriages within a five month period. These were crushing blows to her faith and to her theology. She lost all hope in God for a time, and became almost suicidal. She was angry she had given her trust to a God that didn't come through when things got tough. She was heartbroken.

Meanwhile, I limped along trying to support her, and deal with my own grief at the same time. I didn't have pat answers for her questions, or magical scriptures to fix her emotions. All I had was the sense that I was to be "like Jesus" for her. This meant sharing the pain, and "mourning with those who mourn," and becoming "familiar with sorrows." She cried, I held her, and added a few tears of my own.

I became much closer to Jesus during this period. And I realized that God was speaking to us throughout this trial on numerous levels. I sensed God preparing us for His greater purposes. He was teaching me about compassion. He was calling Suzi to a Job-like state of brokenness, and a direct, Job-like encounter with Him (see Job 42:5). He was refining our "fair-weather" faith and theology. He was challenging us to believe – by faith – that "all things (really) do work together for the good of those who love God and are called according to His purposes."[17]

Despite all this, however, there came a day when doubt and despair overwhelmed me. My universe suddenly became dark, godless, and void of all meaning. My Christianity became utterly foolish and vain. I swirled

---

[17] Romans 8:28

downward in an endless spiral of questions without answers. Angry and depressed, I imagined a future of devout atheism. I ran back and forth in my mind, desperately searching for true reality.

What saved me was Jesus. I kept tripping over Him! He was a stumbling block to my unbelief. He had lived and died and yes, He had risen again. He had revealed a loving, living God. I couldn't deny this truth. He had done too much in my life to discount. I couldn't deny Jesus. In fact, everywhere I turned, I found Him! The answer to every question I raised was Jesus! My faith wouldn't die. Somehow it grew even stronger.

After I emerged from this crisis, I recalled how Jesus had once told Peter,

> "Behold, Satan has demanded permission to sift you like wheat; but I have prayed for you, that your faith may not fail."[18]

This reminds us that our walk of faith includes Satanic challenges, which we'll discuss in a later chapter. But ultimately, Jesus is praying that our faith will not fail. Therefore we must know, like Peter (and Job), that there exists a spiritual reality "behind the scenes," which we can't comprehend. Hence, we can only feebly speculate about "why" things happen.

Ultimately, Suzi (like Job) got a new revelation of God, found only through suffering and disappointment. She got a different, more real relationship with the Father who

---

[18] Luke 22:31

gives and takes away according to His mysterious, yet perfect purposes. And she learned in a most curious way that He is faithful, not necessarily to fix her every problem, or spare her all pain, but to embrace her with His love and comfort in every situation.

As a result of Suzi's miscarriages and the trials of faith which followed, we gained new direction. We sensed that God was calling us to *act* on our long-felt desire to adopt or care for needy children. Another natural-born child in our family would have indefinitely postponed this call on our lives. So through our circumstances, tragic and painful as they were, God was at work, guiding us toward His glorious good pleasure and His perfect will.

Today we're raising a wonderful orphan child born addicted to drugs, and since miraculously delivered from their effects, because our faith was stretched, tested and almost broken by circumstances. We need to hear our Father's voice through circumstances.

OUR COUNSELORS

We also need to keep our ears open for God speaking through counselors. The Bible says that, "in a multitude of counselors there is victory." There is also great wisdom and balance to be found in the counsel of mature men and women. When we seek counsel, we allow God to speak through the gifting and experience of others. We allow God to give us new perspective about ourselves, our circumstances and Him.

Seeking and receiving God's word through the counsel of others requires humility and faith. It requires humility because we must expose, and even submit ourselves to others. We must admit we don't "know it all" and that we need help. It also requires faith to believe that God will speak through the people in our lives.

To "those who have ears to hear," God does speak through people. In fact our Father often prefers this method of revelation because it knits us together. As children of God we're to be not independent, but *inter*-dependent. We're to bear each other's burdens[19] and "speak the truth in love."[20] We're to help each other recognize "blind spots," as well as see strengths and opportunities. We're to encourage and support each other.

In this day of superficial and temporary relationships, we frequently have to make special efforts to obtain counsel. I recently had to schedule appointments with people who know me well enough, and whose perspective I trust enough, to receive counsel. I wanted to get their feedback during an important transition point in my life, and it was well worth it. I heard God's voice confirming certain things and challenging me in other areas, through their counsel. In the process, I was reminded how important it is to cultivate friendships and how much we need each other.

As you seek counsel for the decisions in your life, you'll want to look for people who know God, know scripture and know you. Godly counselors should be honest and loving. If you don't know many such people, pray that God would supply them.

---

[19] Galatians 6:2
[20] Ephesians 4:15

Take another look at your friends, prayer group, church elders, pastor or members of your own family. No matter how long you've walked with God, you need wise counselors around you. Even Moses, a truly great leader, was helped by the counsel of his father-in-law.[21] God speaks – and guides – through counselors.

WALKING TO REST

As we mature in faith and listen for the Father's voice we become more like trusting children. This goes back to Jesus, who said, "unless you are converted and become like children, you shall not enter the kingdom."[22]

As children of God we're called to walk – and *rest* – by faith. In fact, the level of *rest* we enjoy indicates how much we have "grown up" into kingdom maturity.

What does it mean to rest? For one thing it means *relaxing*. This means we stop worrying and trying to "do it all" in our own power. We *can't* do it all. The truth is, we can't do *much* at all! Children instinctively know this. We can only do what Father asks and empowers us to do.

Our efforts to do more than our Father empowers us to do, usually stem from unbelief and are doomed to become wood, hay and stubble on the trash heap of history. The child of faith learns to recognize this, and "let go," as a result. This produces supernatural peace.

As a recovering "go-getter," I've struggled to walk in this mature faith. But I'm improving. As I relax my grip on goals, plans and timing, and entrust more to God, I find

---

[21] Exodus 18:19-27
[22] Matthew 18:3

that His peace fills my life. Stress and anxiety fall away. The simple pleasures of life become pleasurable again. Life itself regains a sense of wonder and awe that vanishes when I "chase after the wind."[23] I've come to agree with king David, who wrote,

> "Commit your way to the Lord, trust also in
> Him and He will do it...Rest in the Lord and
> wait patiently for Him."[24]

Patience flows from a sense of confidence, and confidence is another quality of rest.

To further illustrate, imagine telling a person from a primitive culture without modern transportation that you're going to travel hundreds of miles to another city. Then imagine this person's reaction as you sit down in your car. "Why are you sitting down?" this person might ask, impatiently. "Shouldn't you get walking?"

"This is a better way," you reply, *confident* that your car can take you where you want to go faster than walking. You've learned to trust your car to do what your legs can't, so you *sit down*. You rest!

The truth is, Father can do incredible things for us if we'll trust in Him. Others may look at us like aliens when we stop hustling and start resting, but the fruit of our faithfulness will ultimately be evident. God does come through. In fact He'll move mountains for us!

I see parallels of this all the time with my children when they want to move a chair or large toy or something

---

[23] Ecclesiastes 2:11
[24] Psalm 37:5-7

beyond their strength. They can push and pull and struggle all they want, but they make little progress. Often they get very frustrated, and may even start to cry. But when they recognize their limitations and ask me for help, I'm able to "move the mountains" for them.

I've also noticed how, as the kids become wiser, they learn to ask for help *sooner* – before they exhaust themselves! They learn what tasks are beyond their abilities, and hence, learn to rest in *my* ability. They learn to ask "Daddy."

I've found this to be a powerful dynamic in my own life, too. It's simple, and it works like this. Let's say I don't like the mean, bitter and feisty lady who lives across the street. Instead of trying to manufacture Christian love for her (which I couldn't do in a million years), I go to God.

I pray, "Abba, Father, You know I don't like the nasty lady across the street. You know I'd like to egg her house sometimes! I confess that *I don't love her*. But I know *You* do. I know You see the pain and rejection she's suffered. I know You love her and want to heal her. So let me rest in Your love for her. Amen." And He moves the mountains every time! (Well, *almost* every time, anyway.)

This process of confession and request works the same way with struggles of all kinds, whether they are struggles with obedience, patience, sacrafice or actual tasks that are too big for us. We just stop and confess, "I can't. But Father, I know you can. Will you?" This is "rest faith" at work.

FAITH TO STEP

I've emphasized rest faith because we live in such a "do-do" world. Most of us struggle with letting go, more than with getting going. We've been trained to charge ahead and "take the bull by the horns," without waiting for God. As a result, action comes more naturally to us than rest. So I've hammered away on rest.

<u>But there is a balance</u>. Sometimes we have to act, to plan, to step forward, *in faithfulness* to God. This means asking, "Has Father given ME something to do?" "Is there a step He's waiting for ME to take?" For scaredy cats, procrastinators and perfectionists who tend to "rest" too much, forever waiting for divine intervention, stepping forward may be a greater challenge than resting.

"Faith to step" is *practical* faith that trusts God has given us common sense and the laws of nature, such as sowing and reaping. This is a responsible faith that doesn't leave *everything* in God's hands.

If I'm out of money and have no job, for instance, this faith prompts me to *actively seek* employment, because I have faith enough to step out, to put myself on the line. It's having faith that God will honor my effort to "do the right thing." This faith leads me to work *and* pray, rather than just pray alone for miraculous provision.

In other words, God calls me to faithfully DO what I can do and should do, as a "partner."

I identify quite often with Joshua, the leader who followed Moses and took the Israelites into the Promised Land. God gave him divine promises and guidance, but He also told him to "be strong and courageous,"[25] and required him to fight – not just in prayer, but in flesh and blood! Joshua needed faith that God would do His part, if he would faithfully do his. As children of God, you and I are called to live in this same balance.

Now finally, let me encourage you to establish a history of faith.

A HISTORY OF FAITH

Do you have a spiritual "scrapbook?" A royal family "photo album?" A personal journal? If you don't, let me tell you why you should.

When you keep a record of the special dates, events and insights of your life with God, you build your faith – both as you collect and record these precious things, and later, when you review them.

I've found that as I document my daily or weekly highlights with God, be they miraculous events or simple observations, I become connected with the past and future. I cultivate an attitude of remembrance that is part of my heritage, dating back to Jesus,[26] and Israel's Exodus.[27] When I record my "God stories," I find I'm more likely to remember them – and share them with other people. And this builds the faith of others.

Remembering can also create valuable traditions. Each year on the eve of my birthday, for instance, I've made a tradition of reading my journal from the past year. And

---

[25] Joshua 1:6-7
[26] Luke 22:19-20
[27] Exodus 13:1-10

each year I'm greatly inspired as I review God's deeds in my life – the growing and learning, the miracles, the setbacks and the breakthroughs. I've found that looking back always excites me about moving forward in faith.

And when times get rough, my attitude of remembrance helps helps me to see my life as an adventure, as a tapestry connecting past events with future ones, or a book with many chapters. I remember that Father has come through before, and know that He will again. I know from past (documented!) experiences, that His love never fails. And because I keep track of His activity in my life, I can often sense how He's at work perfecting His purposes in me.

So let me urge you, brother or sister of faith, to cultivate an attitude of remembrance. Start writing notes in a journal. Cultivate traditions and celebrate God's deeds. Remember to look back, then step forward on your adventure of faith.

Here's a prayer to help you on your way.

Thank you, Abba Father, for the life of
faith you've called me to live. Thank you
for your loving guidance and correction.
Please remove my unbelief, and give me ears
to hear your voice – and obey it. Help me to
rest *and* step, and grant me wisdom me to know
when to do which. Increase my faith! And help
me to make history with you, Father, in Jesus'
name. Amen.

CHAPTER SIX

Child of Inheritance

"It's the blessing of the Lord that makes rich."
– Proverbs 10:22

I grew up with a grandmother who drove a Rolls Royce, wore big diamond rings and lived just up the street from the mansion used on *The Beverly Hillbillies* television show. She had servants, travelled the world and owned thoroughbred race horses.

Despite all this however, she was very poor. When I think back about her, I realize that her life was filled with loneliness, insecurity, vanity, anger, prejudice and pride. She never experienced righteousness, peace or joy in the Holy Spirit. In many ways, she lived her life as a slave, bound by the false promises of the world. She lived as a member of Adam's family.

Since my childhood, I've gotten to know many other "rich" people. And I've come to realize how *few* of them are truly "blessed," or happy. Most of them live in the shackles we talked about in chapter one. Shame, fear, denial, jealousy and pain. Many are "driven," but few understand "rest." Many live fragmented lives, while few are whole. Many think money can buy love and approval, but few know they are free gifts from God.

I was reminded of this the other day, when a man came to our door in search of donations for a local food bank. After I gave him a check and a glass of water, we talked for some time on my front steps. One thing he mentioned really caught my attention. He said, "the richer the neighborhood, the more doors are slammed in my face." After he left, I couldn't help reflecting upon his statement.

How could it be that people with the *most* to give, are the *least* willing to? Are they so possessed by their possessions, so fearful of losing what they have, so lost in their pursuit of the "good life," that they live miserable, door-slamming ones?

I recalled that statistics from the Internal Revenue Service found that high income people give *less than* 2% of their income to charity, while the lowest income people give *more than* 5%. And I remembered a story a Christian brother once told me about a mercy outreach to the poor.

He and a group of Christians had prepared bag lunches, and were visiting a vacant lot in Los Angeles where Hispanic immigrants lived together in trash-built shacks. The Christians went door to door giving away the food and blessing people with the gospel of Jesus Christ and with prayer. At one memorable door, they encountered some confusion. They tried to tell the man there that they were giving away food, but he didn't understand.

Suddenly, he motioned for them to wait, and retreated inside. He returned several minutes later with a frown on his face, holding a plastic bag containing a small amount of rice. As he handed it over to the group, he tried to apologize for not having more to give. All his family had was in the bag.

Can you imagine our brother's shock? Here's the "poor" man, giving out of his *poverty*, showing his true wealth! Who's rich and who's poor? I'm coming to some new conclusions, and I hope you will, too. "Blessed are the poor in spirit," said Jesus, "for theirs is the kingdom of heaven."[1]   How much we have to learn about God's blessing, true wealth and our inheritance as children of God.

JUST "PIE IN THE SKY?"

As a child of God, you've received the world's greatest inheritance. The apostle Peter understood this and wrote,

> "Blessed be the God and Father of our Lord Jesus Christ, who...has caused us to be born again...to obtain an inheritance which is imperishable and un- defiled and will not fade away, reserved in heaven for you."[2]

This impacts me in a special way because I once thought "heaven" was just a pathetic concept, a "crutch" to help poor people get through life. A false hope for otherwise hopeless people. Just "pie in the sky." But now I know better.

---

[1] Matthew 5:3
[2] I Peter 1:3-4

I know that when I go to heaven I'll enter into the presence and radiance of Christ.[3] I'll be overwhelmed by His glory. In a flash, in a twinkling of an eye, in a split second my resurrection body will be swallowed up in Christ's victory over death![4] I'll enjoy eternal life in God's love![5]

Does anyone care? Today you have to wonder. Years ago, in the days of "old time religion," people cared about eternity. They were *forced* to care, because sickness and death were everyday realities they couldn't ignore. The grim reaper was very real.

Today we hide and deny death. We focus on the "here and now." We avoid uncomfortable subjects like death and judgment. As a result, eternal life in heaven doesn't pull much weight with people these days.

But I know at least one man who appreciates the value of eternal life today – a friend of mine named Bob. As a middle-aged and quite prosperous Hollywood writer, Bob rejected Jesus and any notion of eternal issues. He had all he needed – a pretty wife, a nice car and a house at the beach. But then one morning, he suffered a massive heart attack while he was out jogging. By the time paramedics reached him, he was clinically dead. Fortunately, they were able to restart his heart and get him to the hospital.

When he finally regained consciousness, Bob flailed his arms and screamed like a madman. He cried out for a Bible and Jesus, desperate to find eternal life – and escape from what he'd experienced in death. He recalls visiting a dark, disgusting and totally hopeless place where violence

---

[3] Romans 8:17-18, Colossians 3:4
[4] I Corinthians 15:35-54
[5] John 3:16,36

and sexual perversion reigned supreme. There were groans of agony and despair. Doom, gloom and rage dominated Bob's senses. It was the bottomless pit of hell, and he didn't want to go back there.

Jesus described this terrible place in His story of The Rich Man and Lazarus.[6] He warned people to seek God, and avoid hell.[7] Hell was even part of His Sermon on the Mount.[8] But as much as He spoke of hell, Jesus preferred talking about eternal life.

"I tell you the truth," He promised, "whoever hears my word and believes Him who sent me has eternal life, and will not be condemned."[9] Paul echoed this when he wrote, "The gift of God is eternal life in Christ Jesus our Lord."[10]

A SLICE OF THE PIE — NOW!

A large and wonderful inheritance is definitely something to look forward to, isn't it? Imagine being an heir to millions of dollars. Wouldn't the very knowledge of it, no matter how long you had to wait, give you hope? Wouldn't it give you a sense of security and confidence about your future? I'm sure it would.

The one thing I've observed among wealthy heirs is their (financial) confidence toward the future. They don't have to worry about things the way "regular" people do. They're "set for life!" They can relax.

---

[6] Luke 16:19-31
[7] Luke 12:5 and Matthew 18:9
[8] Matthew 5:22, 29
[9] John 5:24
[10] Romans 6:23

And so can you, as a child of God. Your future is assured. Jesus said, concerning heaven,

> "Trust in God; trust also in me. In my Father's house are many rooms, if it were not so, I would have told you. I am going there to prepare a place for you."[11]

This is the place where you will endure no more suffering or pain, no more discouragement or tears.[12] You'll literally *bask* in God's love. Everything will be new – and it will stay that way for eternity!

Do you believe Jesus? Sometimes I struggle to. I've learned to measure my level of faith by asking myself *how I feel about dying*. What emotions do I experience when I consider dying today or tomorrow? Anxiety? Or peaceful anticipation?

If I'm walking in doubt, then I get uptight. I find myself *clinging* to things and people, and life itself. But if I'm walking in the Spirit with Father, I'm easygoing. I realize I'm an alien just passing through! And I remember a girl named Candy.

A Christian brother and friend told me about Candy when he related the death of his young daughter. His little girl, along with two other girls, died in a fire when their camp cabin went up in flames. Several of the older girls escaped, including Candy, who was nine. After escaping, a strange thing happened. Candy stopped and looked, then ran *back* into the flames. Fortunately a man pulled her out of the fire

---

[11] John 14:1-2
[12] Revelation 21:4

before she was severely burned.

Afterward, my friend visited the room where Candy was being treated, and was instantly struck by a bright aura of peace surrounding her. She was radiant. He couldn't help asking her, "Candy, why did you run back? Did you think you could save the girls?" But she shook her head, "no." My friend and the other adults were puzzled. Gently, he prodded, "Well, then why did you run back?" She answered quietly, yet matter-of-factly. "I saw Jesus holding the other girls, and I wanted to be with Him, so I ran."

If only we, like Candy, could see Jesus as He is! Standing in glory, radiating love so intense it can draw us through flames! Love so powerful it can lift our eyes beyond suffering and troubles, and fill us with over-flowing confidence! Love so complete it makes us utterly rich! What an experience.

Did you know you can "taste" this experience now, *without* running through flames, and *before* you get to heaven? That you can have a "slice" of heaven's pie, right here on earth? Well it's true, you can! How? Through "interest payments" available through the Holy Spirit.

The Bible says the Holy Spirit was given to us as a "pledge" or down payment, of our royal inheritance.[11] He reveals to us "what is to come," and always spreads the glory of Jesus.[12] He testifies that we are true heirs, through our adoption in Christ,[13] and makes Christ alive *in us*, "the hope of glory."[14] In other words, the Holy Spirit acts like an "allowance" from our trust fund!

---

[11] Ephesians 1:13-14
[12] John 16:13-14
[13] Romans 8:17
[14] Colossians 1:27

Are you receiving it? Are you enjoying it? Are you spending it on others? Glory, glory, glory, you are rich beyond measure!

When you pray, when you worship, when you *allow* the Holy Spirit to raise up living water within you, you become a fountain of wealth! A wellspring of blessing! A rich, rich kingdom kid! No matter what your circumstances, God's heavenly love and joy is waiting – just about bursting – to get out. My prayer for you is that you'll let it flow!

THE FINE PRINT

As a child of God and "co-heir" with Christ, there's just one more thing you should know about. Your inheritance includes some "fine print" some preachers don't want to talk about.

You see, all is not sunshine and spring flowers in the kingdom of God. I must tell you that Jesus promised more than heaven and the Holy Spirit. In fact, He promised you a hard time.

"You will be hated by all, on account of my name," said Jesus,[15] adding,

> "If you belonged to the world, it would love you as its own. As it is, you do not belong to the world, but I have chosen you out of the world. That is why the world hates you."[16]

Great news, huh? And yet there's more.   Paul

---

[15] Matthew 10:22
[16] John 15:19

assured us that, "Everyone who wants to live a godly life in Christ will be persecuted."[17]

Why all the hatred and rejection? The answer lies in the difference between life and death, rich and poor. You see, in the kingdom of God you have abundant life now and eternal life later. In the world, people have spiritual death now and eternal seperation later.

In the new order of life in God's kingdom, you are rich. In the fallen order of the world, people are poor. So it's obvious why we can expect some conflict, isn't it?

Yes, you can expect to catch some flak. People in the world despise you because you're rich in Christ. Deep in their souls they are envious – and dangerous. You break their rules of "happiness" and "prosperity," and you expose their false illusions of "the good life." The bottom line is, you're a child of inheritance, and they're not.

We'll talk more about this conflict in later chapters. But for now it's enough to understand the basic truth of your inheritance. It's real. It's big. And you can even enjoy some of it today.

Here's a prayer for you to put it all in the bank.

> Thank you, Abba, Father, for making me rich in Christ. Thank you for blessing me with the promise of eternal life in your presence, and for giving me a glimpse of that glory right now.
> I pray for new confidence and joy to be released in my heart. Let it flow! And help me to know that I belong to your kingdom, not to this dying world. In Jesus' name I pray. Amen.

---

[17] II Timothy 3:12

CHAPTER SEVEN

Child of Function

"We are God's workmanship, created in Christ
Jesus to do good works." – Ephesians 2:10

When I was growing up and my father wanted a chore done around our house, he had three choices (because he had three sons). If he wanted the car washed, for instance, his choices looked like this.

If he wanted it done *quickly*, he needed to ask James, my oldest brother. Jim was a "bottom line" kind of guy. Highly efficient, always on the go, very businesslike. He'd wash that car in nothing flat! Today he owns a metal brokerage company.

If he wanted the car washed *perfectly*, then my middle brother, Philip, was his man. Phil was a perfectionist. Meticulous and methodical, he'd get that car so clean you could eat off the air filter! Today he's the financial controller of a real estate company.

And finally, if my father wanted the car *half* washed, then I was his guy! You might say I was easily distracted. There were just so many better things to do than wash a car! Today I'm a writer trying to concentrate on finishing this book.

Our heavenly Father has similar choices to make in our kingdom household of faith. There are literally millions of jobs to do in keeping the Royal Family happy, healthy and *functional*. (Remember, Jesus brought us out of Adam's "dysfunctional" family.) As in my dad's case above, our Father must know who to pick for different tasks, based on our personalities, special abilities and levels of maturity. And, like in most households, EVERYONE must pitch in!

Unfortunately, this isn't happening in God's family today. Many Christians are mere *spectators* who idly watch as their brothers and sisters in "full time ministry" do all the work. These spectators sit around eating junk food, watching TV and making a mess, then can't understand why the place is in such shambles! Meanwhile, the "full timers" can't explain why they feel so unsupported and burned out.

We could say a lot about this problem, and the reasons why it exists. People have written whole books on the subject. But I'd rather talk about the solution, which is simple. <u>As children of God, we need to understand how our Father empowers us to serve Him and each other – how we're each called to function in a special way</u>.

As you'll discover in the following pages, it's exciting to learn how and where you fit into the "fabric" of God's family, based on the supernatural abilities you possess in the kingdom. But before we explore these supernatural matters, let me affirm the "natural" abilities you've received from God. What do I mean by "natural?"

I mean things you were born with, the talents, tendencies and interests that were built into you as "standard equipment."

For me, an example would be writing. I've always enjoyed this creative process, which has come quite naturally. As a result, I've written short stories, magazine articles, film and video scripts, speeches and advertising copy over the years.

Yet, in and of itself, my writing ability doesn't serve fellow Christians or glorify God. In fact I've used this gift to serve Walt Disney stockholders and to glorify Mickey Mouse!

I do contribute to society however, through the use of my natural gifting. And so do you. Whether you function as a dancer, doctor or brick layer, an engineer, home-maker or accountant, your natural abilities equip you to contribute.

Your natural abilities also give you great potential to REFLECT God's excellence through your life. If you're a brick layer, for instance, you can lay the best bricks in the world! Then you can give the glory to God, for giving you the ability. Pro athletes and other visible people sometimes do this in interviews.

Because our natural potential is great, you and I need to be good stewards of our gifts. We need to carefully choose how to apply them and how to cultivate them. We need to make the greatest contribution we can with what we've been given. We need to go for it!

We need to use our natural gifts to strengthen the Royal Family, whenever possible. I've written brochures and resumes for Christian brothers, for instance. I know carpenters who have *literally* built up the body of Christ, by doing voluntary or discounted work for others. And I've seen mechanics, financial planners, lawyers and others do the same, using their *practical* ability to help within the church.

These natural abilities are practical but in a sense, they're spiritual, too. They're spiritual because they came from God, who is Spirit.[1] They're spiritual also, because _every_ part of our life reflects our identity as children of God. We can't really divide "spiritual" and "non-spiritual" parts of our lives, as citizens of the kingdom.

SUPERNATURAL GIFTS

But we can specify the _supernatural_ abilities given to us by the Holy Spirit. These abilities are usually called "spiritual gifts."

The apostle Paul wrote, "Now concerning spiritual gifts, brethren, I do not want you to be ignorant."[2] He wanted us to know that the Holy Spirit working in and through us produces ministry which builds up the spiritual health of our family.[3]

These supernatural abilities are available to each of us through the Holy Spirit's indwelling and operation (most often in prayer/worship settings). They're God-given.[4] We can't _manufacture_ them, _buy_ them[5] or _earn_ them through study or training. We can't even _choose_ our spiritual gifts, although we're encouraged to seek the most helpful ones.[6] St. Peter wrote concerning gifts,

---

[1] John 4:24
[2] I Corinthians 12:1
[3] I Corinthians 12:1-31
[4] Romans 12:7
[5] Acts 8:20
[6] I Corinthians 14:39

"Each one (of us) should use whatever gift he
(or she) has received to serve others, faithfully
administering God's grace in its various forms."[7]

In a minute we'll look at the "various forms" mentioned in scripture. But first let me say that when we
"faithfully administer God's grace," God is glorified. In
other words, when we execise our spiritual gifts God gets
immediate credit!

This is very important for us to understand. Take
singers, for instance. One singer may be very talented and
well trained, but not spiritually gifted or surrendered in the
area of worship. So he or she can sing wonderful songs
about Jesus, but people aren't *moved* (supernaturally) to
praise God. They may say, "Boy, she's a good singer," or
"Gee, that was a nice song." But if a different singer is
"anointed" by a functioning spiritual gift, people will have
their eyes lifted and their attention focused upon God.
"Praise God!" They'll say. Do you see the difference?

The same thing applies to teachers. If people leave
a class or church service raving about "our great teacher," or
"our great new insight" instead of "our great God," then you
know something's wrong. The teacher is probably operating in *natural* ability, which can be helpful, but not *supernatural* ability, which builds people's faith and love toward
the Father.

Natural gifts call attention to people, while spiritual
gifts call attention to God, sparking spiritual life in believers. I can't emphasize this enough.

---

[7] I Peter 4:10

We're often misled by credentials and appearances. People are considered "great teachers" because they "know a lot," and have academic degrees to prove it. Others are called "great preachers," because they tell good jokes or speak eloquently.

But the real measurement is the result. Do we end up praising the "eloquent" or "funny" speaker, or God? So remember, <u>effective ministry produces praise and devotion to God</u>.

I learned my lesson about this the hard way a few years ago at a men's retreat. I was out in the forest, walking and talking with a brother, when we stopped to pray. As we did, God used me (in my gifting) to minister to him in a powerful way. He wept as God poured confirmation and direction into his heart. He realized afresh that God had special purposes for his life. It was a great time in the Lord.

The next afternoon he and the rest of our cabin mates gathered to share about the weekend. Each man took a turn saying what the retreat had meant to him. I couldn't wait to hear this brother's report. I knew he'd have to say something about the day before, and of course, something about me, too. I figured he'd say something like, "I really want to thank John for his powerful ministry yesterday. He's an awesome man of God!" So I was on the edge of my seat, waiting for his turn to come.

When he finally spoke, I wanted to scream. He wasn't talking about me at all! I sat there waiting and wondering *when* he was going to mention me. But all he wanted to talk about was *God*. God *said* this, and God *did* that. God, God, God. It was as if he cared more about *God* than me! To my great dismay, he didn't mention a single word about me.

That afternoon I drove the three hour trip home by myself, just me and my bruised ego for company. But of course I wasn't alone. Our Father was there, consoling and instructing me. "You know it's *effective ministry*, son, when I get the glory. If you're getting too much, then watch out."

He impressed me with the notion of *agency*, and left me with the image of a superstar's agent. I realized that the agent enjoys great priviledge and authority, representing the superstar. Yet it's always the superstar's interests that matter, not the agent's. As children of God, we can't forget that we function as our Father's "agents" in ministry, always pursuing His interests.

We also need to remember that God's gifting can come in surprising packages. Prophets, for instance, rarely have seminary Ph.D's. It's not always the pastor who has the gift of exhortation, either. The janitor or grandmother may have it, and will need to be released to minister in it. Meanwhile, the housewife might have the gift of healing, rather than the doctor. This is why we're *all* called to minister, and why we must break the spectator church mold. We can't just sit around, there's too much work to be done!

This is why the small group or "home church" movement is such a healthy development today. Christians who meet together informally are able to function freely and productively.

Our Father has spiritually gifted us to work together in harmony, like obedient children in a household, or musicians in an orchestra. When we free ourselves to function in the gifts, people are encouraged, relationships are strengthened, and our Father is glorified. We all praise God together.

FUNCTIONAL GIFTS

Every child of God is empowered to serve. Jesus said He came "not to be served, but to serve."[8] The apostle Paul exhorted us to *aggressively serve* the Lord and each other "in the newness of the Spirit."[9] The following spiritual gifts help us strengthen the family and glorify the Father. As you read, note which descriptions "fit" you, then note people's reaction to the gift's operation. (These gifts are mentioned in Romans 12:6-8, I Corinthians 12-14 and Ephesians 4:7-13.)

Mercy: This special sensitivity toward the oppressed and downtrodden allows you to serve hurting people with great sympathy. You can make the lowly feel special and loved. People praise God for His mercy.

Caring/Helps: The ability to give emotional and practical assistance, with a joyful heart. You have a supernatural concern for others, and you often *do* something about it, even in small or menial ways. People praise God He cares about the "little" things.

Hospitality: You invite people to visit and make them comfortable enough to express thoughts and emotions about God. You make people feel "at home." People praise God they have a place to come and be blessed.

Serving: Similar to the caring/helps gift, this gift specially equips you for task-oriented ministry. Deacons typically have this gift. You don't need glory or honor, you just want

---

[8] Matthew 20:28
[9] Romans 7:6, 12:11

to do your part and get things done properly. People praise God for His excellence.

Giving: A great awareness of material needs, and a strong desire to meet them, are signs of this gift. Sharing what God has given you is a serious yet joyful ministry for you. People praise God for His provision.

Administration: This involves a special capacity to organize and lead among God's people. You like to manage the details so things run smoothly. People praise God that He brings order (not control!) to chaos.

Faith: This gift enables you to see the adequacy of God to an unusual degree. You're unshakably confident that God can and will come through, so you pray! People praise God He *can* move mountains.

Discernment: The ability to distinguish whether spirits are from God or not. Alarms go off when you hear false teaching or bad doctrine, or when you encounter Satanic oppression. You have a special "nose" for spiritual truth. People praise God for His protection.

Exhortation: This gift enables you to encourage or comfort others in a special way. You motivate people to seek a deeper and more fruitful relationship with God. People praise God He offers abundant life.

Word of Knowledge: This enables you to grasp the truth, especially a fact or detail, about a situation as God sees it. Sometimes you get a flash of insight that only God could know. People praise God He knows everything.

Word of Wisdom: This gift allows you to speak penetrating truth in response to a situation. Sometimes you say things that are simply beyond you. People praise God for His wisdom.

Healing: This gift enables you to act as an instrument of God's healing grace, by prayer, laying on of hands or by commands. Sometimes you pray and God heals 'em! People praise God He heals.

Miracles: God alters, suspends or controls the laws of nature through you. You have witnesses! People praise God for His awesomeness.

Teaching: The special ability to explain scripture to others in an understandable and dynamic fashion. You bring the Bible alive for people who then apply it to their lives. (This is one gift that comes with a warning. Teachers will be judged harshly for leading others astray. Sound doctrine is a must!) People praise God for His word and ways.

Pastoring: This gift enables you to guide people with great care and integrity. (Laypeople with this gift can serve as disciplers or home group pastors.) You want to nurture the people God's given you. People praise God for His loving care.

Evangelism: This is a special ability, either in public or in private, to communicate the good news of Jesus Christ, with good results. You just have a knack for bringing people into the kingdom. (You may also have a knack for encouraging others to share their faith.) People praise God for sending His Son.

Prophecy: Sometimes this gift enables you to "see" a glimpse of future events, due to direct revelation from God. More often, this revelation enables you to speak timely words of confirmation, guidance or correction so that people hear God speaking directly to their situation. People praise God He's alive, involved and communicating. ("Prophetic" people, like Old Testament prophets, are often hell-bent on bringing truth and justice to light, as well. If this describes you, then watch out for flying stones – usually from Comfortable Christians!)

Apostleship: This gift enables you to establish, instruct or oversee local chuches. Effective missionaries and church planters often have this gift, which features the use of numerous functions listed above. You're able – and compelled – to break new ground for Christ's sake, and you expect God to back you with power. People praise God He sends people to expand the kingdom.

Tongues (Public): This sometimes controversial work of the Spirit produces a message as a prayer, song or prophetic "word" in a language you don't know, for others to appreciate by way of an interpretation. You're compelled to speak in tongues, trusting there will be an interpretation. (Without interpretation, tongues are out of order in public, due to their disruptive and confusing nature.[10]) People praise God for His amazing communication.

Interpretation of Tongues: This enables you to hear a message given in a foreign tongue and provide clear interpretation for others. Somehow you know exactly what a tongue-speaking person is saying, and feel compelled to share it with others. People praise God for His ability to turn babble into revelation.

Tongues (Private): You utter words of a "prayer language," known only in heaven, by which you commune or intercede with God. The Holy Spirit overflows, and you release "groanings too deep for words."[11] You praise God for His love and power.

---

[10] I Corinthians 14:23, 39-40
[11] Romans 8:26

Other Gifts: It's possible the Holy Spirit is expressed through Christians in other ways, as well. Some gifts not specifically mentioned in scripture but apparent in history include celibacy, counseling, intercessory prayer, worship and deliverance, to name a few.

FINDING YOUR FUNCTION

So where do you fit in the family? Hopefully one of the gifts described above "had your name on it." Most of us find that *several* gifts apply to us, to one degree or another. We often find the line is blurred between natural and supernatural activity, too. And that's okay.

The ministry of the Holy Spirit isn't "cut and dried" or clearly catagorized. God is not limited. Paul emphasized the Spirit's *various* expressions, not a rigidly itemized few.

I believe that as we walk as children of God, yielded to the Spirit, we can function in most of the ways mentioned above, although certain gifts will tend to dominate in each of us. The important thing, as stated by Paul, is that we *not be ignorant* concerning the gifts. And of course our primary focus isn't on the gifts, but on the *Giver* of gifts, as James, the half brother of Jesus, reminded us,

> "Every good thing bestowed and every perfect gift is from above, coming down from the Father of lights."[12]

---

[12] James 1:17

I want to encourage you to ask Father what gifts He's given you, and how He wants you to use them. As you do, stop and reflect on how He's used you in the past. Look for patterns of spiritual activity. Ask yourself what kind of ministry has given you the most joy in the past, as operating in your gifts is usually very fulfilling.

What's your deepest desire before God? What do you think about most, when you consider the needs of the church? Where do you receive most affirmation from people and God? These are the questions which begin to reveal your Royal Family function, and provide an exciting sense of purpose in your life.

As you consider these questions, just be certain of one thing. God loves you and wants to use you. You are very special and uniquely gifted. Nobody on earth can touch the lives of people and glorify our Father the way you can. There's no competition for your function and you're not meant to be a spectator. You are God's workmanship, created in Christ Jesus to do good works!

And another thing. Please don't try to deny your gifting out of some false sense of humility. It really is okay to affirm your supernatural abilities. We need to know about them, so we can confidently FUNCTION in them, to the service of others and the glory of God!

Think about it. If people tell you, "Praise God, you've got the gift of mercy!" Do you help anyone by denying it? By saying, "Oh, not really. I'm not gifted at all." No!! If their statement is true, don't lie and deny it! If an attractive woman was complimented for her beauty, would you expect her to say, "Oh no, I'm really quite ugly"? Of course not. If she's truly humble, she can simply say,

"Thank you, God's been graceful to me."

See how this works? Denial is *false* humility. Christians often get tangled up in this. "Oh no, I'm just a worthless worm," they say. But <u>true humility acknow-ledges the truth and directs the glory to God</u>. "Yes, God seems to have gifted me," you say. "I just want to be *faithful* with that gift." See?

Giving gifts is our Father's business, while being faithful with them is ours. The first step to being faithful is to discover, then humbly *affirm* what we've received. As we do, we gain the confidence to properly function, which glorifies the Father. A good friend summed it up by saying, "True humility is agreeing with God."

I think this is true. So don't be afraid to affirm the gifts God has given you. And don't be stingy with affirmation of your brothers and sisters, either. Be humble and thankful, and most of all be faithful!

TIME TO FUNCTION

And please be patient. Ask and wait. God will reveal everything to you in His perfect timing. Your particular function may take time to surface as you seek to serve God in different ways. But you can trust that He has a purpose for you right where you're at, and also where you're going.

Sometimes He has to *prepare you for more effective ministry*, by healing, maturing and testing you, too. Like in any family, jobs are given to match your ability and maturity. This process of discovery and growth can take time. Sometimes He'll even wait for you to "die" to ministry in your natural gifting, in order to release His spiritual gifting and call. (God prepared Moses for 40 years!) I know a little about this, myself.

The day I received Christ at the age of 25, I knew I'd been *created* to communicate the gospel. I clearly sensed that I was called to fulfill a special function for God. And after receiving a powerful confirmation through the Holy Spirit a year later I was set to go, guns blazing for Jesus. But I also heard the Father's voice saying, "Slow down, son, nothing special's going to happen until you're 30."

Naturally, I didn't like hearing that at all! I was in no mood to wait several years while the whole world went to hell! So I ignored God's voice, and tried to minister through my own zeal, natural ability and "good ideas." And boy, did I learn the difference between "good ideas" and *God's* ideas.

One event stands out in my mind. It was a great idea – an evangelistic crusade targeting high school athletes in a large section of Los Angeles. With my sports background and connections (I was publishing a sports magazine), it was a "natural." I invited two star football players from USC, Rodney Peete and Eric Affholter, to come and give their testimonies for Christ, then figured I'd reap the masses with an evangelistic message.

I got flyers out to all the school athletic departments to promote it, booked a large church building to host it, then braced for the stampede. But noone came. There may have been 20 people, tops! I wanted to die.

God wanted me to die, too. He wanted to kill off the "old John," and resurrect the new. And apparently He knew it would take a few years! So after a number of other futile attempts at "ministry," I took the hint, crawled into a hole, and died. I decided to focus on my business and just serve in the children's ministry at church. I put away my smoking guns and great ambitions.

But let me tell you, in the period that followed, God taught me about His heart for "the least of these" (i.e. children), about faithfulness in "little things," and about character. He shaped and refined me, without my even knowing it.

When I finally turned 30, I'd forgotten all about His voice and calling. But He reminded me with a bang. He clarified my gifting and started moving with dramatic revelations and affirmations. He started moving me in a new direction – out of the tomb and into kingdom ministry!

Since then, He's continued to shape and refine, heal and expand me. For *His* purposes, *His* ministry, *His* glory, and in *His* perfect timing. This is my prayer. I hope it will be yours, too.

Thank you, Father, for knowing and loving me. Thank you for creating me new in Christ Jesus, to accomplish your good works. Please show me the gifts you've given me, and how I can best use them to serve you, the world and my brothers and sisters. Please help me to perform my special function, by the power of your Spirit, in your perfect timing. In Jesus' name. Amen.

CHAPTER EIGHT

Child of Power

"Power is perfected in weakness." – II Corinthians 12:9

It was just your ordinary garden party. My parents had invited family and friends over to enjoy their newly landscaped yard and a little socializing. Nothing special. So when I stepped out the back door with Suzi and the kids, I had no idea I was heading into a memorable lesson about God's extraordinary power.

But almost immediately, I was intercepted by a woman I didn't know. She was about 60, had silver hair, a friendly smile and was wearing all black. I literally fell into her clutches, as she steered me away from my family. "I've been looking forward to talking with you," she said, as if she knew all about me. "I've got some relatives who believe in the same philosophy you do." Her voice hinted at a challenge. "*Philosophy?*" I replied, my blood pressure rising. "You know," she continued, "your religion."

I spent the next twenty minutes sparring with her, taking questions and comments, like punches. I kept telling her, as politely as I could, that I wasn't *religious*, but that I had a *relationship* with God. I kept trying to focus the conversation on the person of Jesus Christ. But to no avail. She was tough, and she wasn't listening. She was blind to Jesus, and had built up a brick wall toward Christianity. She stubbornly rejected my claims and explanations. Like so many religious debates, our conversation was going no-where.

Finally, I said in my heart, "Father, I give up! What can I say to this woman?"

It was then that He spoke, reminding me of words He'd given me a week earlier, when I'd asked for a "boiled down" gospel presentation. He whispered, "Tell her what I told you." And so I did.

Without thinking, I gently put a hand on her shoulder, gazed into her eyes, and said, "Look, all I can tell you is that Jesus loves you so much He was willing to die for you. And the same power that raised Him from the grave can give you new life."

And she broke! Something deep within her cracked open, releasing sobs, which she tried to suppress, but couldn't. She quickly excused herself and hurried toward the bathroom as tears poured from her eyes. Her husband, who'd been silently watching the whole time, turned and said to me in amazement. "Boy, you sure did it to her!"

"No sir," I replied, "*God* did it to her." He could only shake his head and smile. He was amazed *and* amused. Then, for some reason, I asked, "Does your wife cry like that a lot?" His smile disappeared as he looked at me and said, "She *never* cries."

I still don't know who that lady was. I didn't ask, and I didn't see her again that night, nor have I since. But I do know that God spoke to her with life-changing impact, and probably answered the prayers of her Christian relatives, at the same time. I know that God's power can pierce any wall, and touch any heart, as a result. And I know it all began when I confessed my weakness.

THE ABC'S OF KINGDOM POWER

As a child of God, you have access to *mountain moving* power. You are related to the ultimate creative force in the universe! Like Paul, you can say, "I can do all things through Him who strengthens me."[1]   You can trust Jesus, who said, "Anyone who has faith in me will do what (miracles) I have been doing. He (or she) will do even greater things than these."[2]

But like Paul, you must also know that God's power works through your *weakness*.[3] You must recall that Jesus said, "Apart from me you can do nothing."[4]   You must remember that God's greatest power was unleashed through a Son who surrendered to suffering, humiliation and death on a cross.

So how does God's power work through us? I believe the ABC's of practical kingdom power are found in the words, "STOP, LOOK and LISTEN." In the encounter I described above, I was banging my head against a wall, operating in my own strength. It was only when I STOPPED my efforts, LOOKED to Father for help, and LISTENED for His response, that there was a breakthrough.

Apart from God I was powerless, despite all my theology and persuasive ability. I could do nothing, or very little, on my own. I needed to recall God's word which says,

---

[1] Philippians 4:13
[2] John 14:12
[3] II Corinthians 12:9-10
[4] John 15:5

"Cease striving and know that I am God."[5] I needed to enter the "rest" we talked about back in chapter five. Remember confession and request?   Remember how the wise child learns to ask the Father for help – *before* getting exhausted? Sadly, it was my desperation, not my wisdom, that caused me to STOP. But even so, it's better to STOP late – than never!

The next step was to LOOK. Like Jesus, who LOOKED up to the Father before miraculously breaking bread for the multitudes,[6] I needed to seek God. I needed to follow the Psalmist, who wrote,

> "I lift up my eyes to the hills – where does my
> help come from? My help comes from the
> Lord, the maker of heaven and earth."[7]

When I finally stopped and LOOKED to our Father for help, I was on the right track. I was going to the *source* of all power.

The last "power step" was to LISTEN. God could have said anything, or nothing. If He had said nothing, hopefully I would have excused myself from the debate and "agreed to disagree." But He did speak.

Although His voice is rarely as clear as we'd like it to be, it still can make an impression, through the Holy Spirit – if we're LISTENING! We can usually hear well enough to respond. Because I was *desperately* LISTENING, I heard

---

[5] Psalm 46:10

[6] Matthew 14:19

[7] Psalm 121:1

and could obey. I acted upon the impression He gave me (which always involves some risk), and watched it hit the "bull's eye."

The first time I encountered this approach was back in 1986, at a conference Suzi and I attended with some people from our church. One morning during a time of small group ministry, we were encouraged to pray for physical healing. The only person in our group with an ailment was Cindy, a woman in her mid-thirties. She had neck and back problems serious enough to warrant therapy.

And so we started praying for Cindy with great enthusiasm, totally focused on her problem. We prayed loud and hard, almost with smoke coming out of our ears! She gritted her teeth in faith. We laid hands on her, while asking God for a miracle. We did this for about five minutes, never STOPPING to ask our Father for guidance.

I then noticed a young man, kind of hovering nearby, observing. He quietly approached, and asked if he could join us in prayer. I said, "Sure." Because we were all exhausted, we let him take over. He touched her neck, paused a moment, then said God wanted to heal her. He made specific reference to a particular vertebra in her neck, and she almost fainted! In that instant, she realized God knew her exact medical condition, and it wiped her out. After a moment, she collected herself and stood up, *relieved of all neck pain*, sharing how his prayer had hit her X-ray diagnosis right on the nose!

Later, this young man explained that God had gifted him in healing and words of knowledge. The key was to STOP, LOOK and LISTEN. As he waited and watched people minister throughout the conference hall, he listened for guidance. And God steered him to us. He had functioned in his gifting, God had moved in power, and we (*especially* Cindy) had praised God.

Now let me share a few more notes on this "power process."

INCREASE – DECREASE

John the Baptist proclaimed, "He (Jesus) must increase, but I must decrease."[8] He recognized the awesome work and power of God in Jesus, and knew he had to step aside for that power to go forth. His function was to faithfully introduce God's power to people, then let God take care of the rest. As children of God, that's our function, too.

We must *yield* and *trust* and *surrender* and become *dependent* upon our Father. This unleashes the Holy Spirit in our lives, bringing wholeness and love to us, and blessing to others. We must *decrease* for the power of God to increase. It's really that simple.

Yet many Christians doubt this power, and won't decrease. Sure, they believe God's power parted the Red Sea, but they doubt it can put their marriages back together. They know it could heal lepers way back when, but they're not so sure what it can do now.

Our problem today is that we've bought the ultimate lie. We think our techniques, formulas and programs can save us. We trust education and human wisdom more than God. We forget that "The kingdom of God consists NOT in

---

[8] John 3:30

words, but in power."[9]

In our seminaries and church organizations we salute knowledge and scholarship. We judge people by their educational credentials. But this is utterly wrong. Jesus, who possessed no formal training or credentials, shocked a group of stiff-necked religious scholars, by telling them, "You are wrong, because you do not know the scriptures or the power of God."[10] These guys *memorized* scripture, they were the "experts!" But they didn't know God's power. They needed to *decrease*.

I'm convinced God will move in power as we move our thick heads out of the way! If we'll stop relying on *what* we know, and start relying on *who* we know, God's power will flow! Religion is powerless and burdensome. But God's power can save, deliver, heal, forgive, overcome, refresh, comfort and provide! As God's children, we can boast in a Father who can do it all.

UNLIMITED POWER

My friend and brother, Jim Love, has experienced God's power. Once a big-time drug trafficker, Jim was rescued by Jesus Christ. Not just from a life void of meaning, but from death, three times. (He was literally "code blue" each time.) Today he runs a car repair business and lives a life surrendered to the Father, who has gifted him prophetically and evangelistically.

---

[9] I Corinthians 4:20
[10] Matthew 22:23-33

Just the other day he told me of a powerful experience. As he was LISTENING to God's voice, he got a word for one of his employees, a young gang member. Jim had been telling the young man about Jesus, and trying to talk him out of his gang activities, but with little effect. Then he received a word from God. "You're going to get shot," he told the young man, "but God's going to spare you, so you can receive Jesus."

Three days later the employee was shot in the chest. Rather than kill him, the bullet bounced off a rib and came back out! Needless to say, he believed in Jesus and is now growing in faith.

My wife Suzi and I have witnessed God's powerful deliverance. The first time was when our son, A.J., was about two. We became deeply concerned about him, because every time we stopped to pray before meals, he started to fuss. It was consistent, frustrating and very strange. He'd actually say, "No!" Then he'd twist and turn defiantly. He didn't like hearing Bible stories, either.

I suggested that we pray for him, and so we did. But rather than offer up our own weak words, we STOPPED, LOOKED and LISTENED. We confessed, "Father, we have no idea what's going on here. Can You help us?" Suzi then received the word, "discontentment." So, in the name of Jesus Christ, I commanded the evil spirit of discontentment to leave. For a moment, A.J. twisted and strained, while his eyes literally rolled up into his sockets! I repeated this command, then watched my son relax. Everything came back to normal. And from that moment to this, he has joyfully prayed, sung and talked about Jesus. God's power worked through our weakness.

Several months ago, we saw this power and gifting work again, this time with a very troubled adult member of our home fellowship, named Dennis. It was on Good Friday night, after we had worshipped and taken communion together. We were just about to close our meeting, when one discerning sister asked Dennis if we could pray for him.

Although he was reluctant, he finally said, "okay." As we prayed for him, STOPPING, LOOKING and LISTENING, Suzi received a word regarding witchcraft. As I prayed against this evil spirit, God had me guide Dennis through a process in which he renounced witchcraft and other occultic activities he'd been involved in, and then repeated a number of positive confessions about his deliverance and adoption through Jesus Christ.

During this powerful time of ministry, Suzi called attention to a native American necklace Dennis was wearing, representing an eagle god, and asked if he would surrender it. He said he would. Then, just as I told him we would try to replace it with a cross, a visiting brother stepped forward to offer his own crucifix necklace to Dennis, symbolically sealing the conversion.

When the evening was over, Dennis was a new man. Joy was overflowing from him. We were shocked by his bright smile. He'd been laboring under a dark cloud of spiritual oppression for years, even while a professing Christian, and suddenly he was in God's radiant light! He was beaming! And in the weeks and months since then, his life has miraculously turned around in every area; work, relationships and health. We are watching the power of God transform him. Praise God!

(If you are unfamiliar with the kind of ministry described in these testimonies, and want to know more about it, you're in luck. We'll talk about spiritual warfare in chapter eleven.)

God's power can refresh, too. I remember talking with a youth pastor friend of mine, named Jim, one day when he looked defeated. He was telling me how hard he'd been working and how tired he was getting. So I offered to pray for him. I prayed for God's strength and encouragement in him, but felt my words were pathetic and empty. Just another token prayer. Finally I STOPPED, LOOKED and LISTENED. I asked, "Father, what do You see here? What can I say?"

Suddenly I had a vision of a waterfall. So I started telling Jim what I thought God was showing me, and as I spoke, more prophetic insights came. The message for Jim was that he needed to come under the covering of God, to that protected place under the cliff, *behind the waterfall*, where the Holy Spirit, like mist, would refresh him.

Jim seemed much better after hearing this, but he was silent, as if lost in his own little world. I wondered whether God had actually spoken to him, or if the waterfall was a product of my own imagination. So I asked him.

He explained that he was amazed. In his work as a surf photographer, he'd travelled the world and stood behind *many* waterfalls. More than most people, he knew *exactly* how awesome and wonderful it was to enjoy the cool mist in that special place. And only God knew that he knew! So he was praising God for calling him into that special – and personal – place of refreshment. God's power was very real for him, and for me.

I've seen God's power bring emotional comfort and healing, too. I remember sitting in a church service several years ago, watching as people in the congregation stood up to signal their need of prayer. The pastor then encouraged others nearby to minister to them. I felt a prompting to pray for someone, but the people standing in my area were all taken care of. So I STOPPED to look around the room, and saw a middle-aged woman standing alone, quite a distance away.

My initial perception was that she needed ministry from a woman or older person, and that she might turn away from somebody like me. But as I LOOKED and LISTENED to Father, His will was clear. I was to risk rejection and embarrasment, and go to her.

When I reached her and opened my arms toward her, she broke into tears and desperately hugged me. The Holy Spirit was already doing a deep work, all I needed to do was hold and reassure her as she cried and cried. I kept asking, "Father, how should I pray for this precious woman?"

The only thing that came to mind was the woman who was healed by touching Jesus' robe, recounted in Mark 5:25. And so I quietly reminded her of this story, which made her break up even more! She was practically wailing.

Later, after she had calmed down, the woman confided that she had been a child victim of incest, and that she had yearned for the Father's safe and reassuring touch, ever since. She had felt that in my arms, she said, and had experienced a deep healing. But more than that, she knew God heard her prayers, because that very morning she had cried out, "If only I could touch the hem of your garment, Lord, I'd be healed!" And so she was.

This process of STOPPING, LOOKING and LIS-
TENING unleashes God's power to overcome sinful habits
and addictions in our lives, too. The success of 12-step
recovery programs, like Alcohlics Anonomous, is at least
partly linked to this process. Their very first step is to admit
their *powerlessness*. People STOP trying to "do-it-them-
selves." And what a powerful step this is! Especially when
the Holy Spirit's involved.

This isn't just for drug and alcohol addictions, either. Eating, spending, sexual and other addictions are
broken with the same first step. "Father, I can't overcome
this thing by myself," we confess. "I'm powerless against
it." Then we LOOK for God's supernatural assistance, and
LISTEN for His answer.

One habit I've battled for many years is chronic
tardiness, or being late. I've turned over "new leafs," set
"New Year's resolutions," and failed miserably with each
new effort. I know there are various issues involved, like
control, rebellion and self-deception. But what finally
helped me was STOPPING. "Father, I quit," I confessed.
"My efforts at being on-time don't work. This pattern is too
deeply ingrained for me to overcome on my own."

I then LOOKED for His heavenly power. "Will you
do a work in me to change this?" I asked. And then I
LISTENED. His answer has come with a powerful new
attitude rising up within me. This attitude celebrates the joy
and peace of *being early*. Somehow God has changed my
wiring all around. Now I actually look forward to being *on
time* – at the very latest! No, I haven't become perfect in this,
but His power is perfecting me.

I know His power can transform you, too. From the inside out. I've seen it happen in people struggling with everything from smoking to masturbation. Whatever you're struggling with, turn it over to God. Let *His* power do the work. Be faithful in every part of your life. Open yourself to His healing, transforming power. It starts with STOPPING, and it continues with,...well, you know how it goes after that.

MORE POWER

There are so many stories I could tell about God's power working through His children. People just like you. Take the story of Irene. Her 20 year old daughter had just broken up with her boyfriend, an angry and violent young man. During their relationship, he had physically abused her. And now, he was threatening to kill her. One night a bullet shattered a window in their house. He was terrorizing them on the phone, too. It became so frightening, the daughter fled to another state.

Then one night, Irene answered the phone and, instead of hanging up, paused to pray. "Father, how can I get out of this nightmare?"

She didn't like God's answer. "*Forgive* him??" She protested. "He's a maniac. He should be behind bars! I *can't* forgive him," she said.

But God assured her that forgiveness was His supernatural answer to her problem. So finally she relented. "Okay, Lord, but *You* do it."

And God did, through the Holy Spirit. He strengthened her and gave her the words to say. She told the violent young man that despite everything God loved him and she forgave him. She talked and talked, telling him about the love and power of Jesus Christ. And he listened in stunned silence. He'd never heard anything like it! He was encountering God's power perfected in weakness, and it was blowing him away!

After that night, their phone calls continued. They talked about Jesus. Despite her fear and anger, Irene ministered to the young man. Soon he was joining her at church, confessing Christ as his Savior. The daughter came home, and the young man moved out of town a new man, radically transformed by an awesome God.

Just the other day we heard another powerful story, from a sister and friend named Twinkle. She called us to report a healing. A few days earlier she had prayed for a woman who was diagnosed with a grapefruit sized tumor and was scheduled for surgery. The woman's doctor had given her drugs to reduce the tumor's size, but when she came to him after prayer the tumor was *completely gone*. He cancelled the surgery and called it a miracle.

Doubting that God had done the work and not the drugs, the woman questioned her doctor's statement. He simply responded, "Ma'am, this is my specialty. I've been doing this for 20 years. So you can believe me when I tell you – it's a miracle!" She now believes in God's power, while our sister Twinkle wants to pray for everyone. Praise God!

We experienced something just as dramatic, when we brought our foster child home from an abandoned children's shelter. He was three months old, and had just recovered from the effects of his mother's drug abuse. She had used crack, heroine and alcohol, even on the night of his emergency delivery.

Although he had gone through detoxification by the time we picked him up, his arms and legs were still rigid and stiff. The social workers told us to massage his body in the coming months to make his muscles more limber.

But the second night we had him, God did something powerful. Suzi was holding him, while listening to worship music in our living room. She wept as she prayed in tongues for God to touch him. And then, pow! He suddenly jerked, almost out of her hands! It was like a violent jolt. She felt that God's power had coursed through his little body, setting him free.

When I got home, she showed him to me and asked if I could see any difference.

"Of course I can," I answered in amazement, "his arms used to be like pipes, and his fingers were crunched into fists. But now look – they're totally loose!"

And they were. His body was flexible and normal, and it has been ever since. The doctors say he's perfectly healthy, with no signs of drug impairment whatsoever. We praise God for His deliverance and healing power.

Now why doesn't God heal *all* tumors and *all* crack babies? I don't know. I can't even speculate. There's so much I can't figure out about God. All I know it that the Lord once asked Abraham, "Is anything too difficult for God?"[11] And like him, I know the answer is, "No, *nothing* is too difficult for God."

---

[11]Genesis 18:14

I've seen him miraculously provide *freighters* for a brother who runs an international mercy ministry. And I've seen him provide homes, cars, trucks, airline tickets, jobs, money, food and much more for other brothers and sisters seeking to do His will. I'm convinced that "all things are possible" with our Father.[12] He can and will provide.

To prove my point, let me tell you one final story – a story about beef. It was during my first summer at seminary that I complained to Suzi. We were eating dinner when I told her I was getting tired of eating chicken *every night*. "I can't remember the last time we had steak," I said. "It would sure be nice to taste a big T-bone!"

"Well, it would be nice to have more money, too!" She shot back. Needless to say, I didn't get very far with the topic that night.

But for some reason the idea of eating beef became very important to me during the next two days. I was practically salivating for steak! I couldn't shake my craving for it. I found myself talking to God about it, too. "Father," I said, "I know I should be grateful for *any* food You give me, even chicken every night. People are starving all over the world. I know that. And I know I'm selfish even thinking about steak. But even so, I really would like some beef! Any chance You could help?" I left my request in His hands.

His response came the following evening when I was out working in my front yard. Suzi and the kids were keeping me company when a speeding truck screetched to a stop just beyond our driveway. It backed up slowly, then

---

[12] Mark 14:36

produced a smiling man who got out and approached me. "Do you eat beef?" He asked. "Funny you should ask!" I replied, with a curious expression on my face.

He opened the back of his freezer truck and explained why it was loaded with restaurant quality steak and seafood. "I have a monthly route to private, wholesale customers in the area," he said. "But I've got extra, if you'd like to buy some cheap."

Thirty minutes later our freezer was jammed full of Filet Mignon, T-bone and Spencer steaks, along with some beautiful Lobster, Shrimp and Halibut!

Yes, God had moved in power. And just to confirm it, the meat man stayed to talk with me for over two hours – all about Jesus. As hungry as I was for beef, he was that hungry to hear about the Lord. We both got our fill that night, thanks to an awesome God whom you and I call, "Abba, Father." Here's a prayer.

> Father, I believe that all things are possible
> with you, according to your perfect will.
> I know you can work miracles in every
> situation, if I'll STOP, LOOK and LISTEN.
> Help me to decrease, surrender and yield
> so that your power might increase! I pray
> this all in Jesus' mighty name. Amen.

CHAPTER NINE

Family Policy

"Love your enemies, do good to those who hate you,
bless those who curse you." – Luke 6:27-28

As adopted children of God, we need to realize our Father isn't a Democrat or a Republican, a conservative or a liberal, a communist or a capitalist. He's not American or European, African or Asian. He doesn't belong to our organization, or necessarily share our opinion. The truth is, He doesn't fit our categories at all!

"My thoughts are not your thoughts, my ways are not your ways,"[1] He declares. "My kingdom is not of this world,"[2] said Jesus.

Obviously, we've got a lot to learn about the kingdom. We've been raised and trained in the world, and "naturally" represent the ways of Cain and Abel, Adam and Eve. Our minds are crammed full of fallen "facts," vain philosophies and twisted prejudices. We've been indoctrinated by scientists, teachers, politicians and advertisers since the day we were born. Even our religious attitudes have been distorted by our culture. As a result, we need to be reprogrammed, retrained and spiritually *brainwashed*!

---

[1] Isaiah 55:8
[2] John 18:36

In order to represent our Father, and live as "ambassadors for Christ,"[3] we need a clear revelation of His kingdom. How do we gain this revelation? Mostly we pray. "Father, give us Your heart. Give us Your mind. Show us Your kingdom!" But we also need to ask questions and take notes from the Crowned Prince, Jesus, who *demonstrated* the kingdom for us. We need to learn the "ropes" of Royal Family policy from Him.

Where do we start? We start (and end) with love. Remember, it's the Father's love that sent Jesus to us in the first place. It's the Father's love, like warmth and light itself, that reached into our hearts to set us free. It's the Father's love that filled and adopted us, through the Holy Spirit. This is supernatural love. The kind that reaches out to enemies, outcasts and unlovely rebels. The kind that forgives and heals and offers hope.

We see this love when we look at Jesus. We see it at His baptism, when He identified Himself with lowly sinners like you and me. We see it in His temptation, when He rejected economic, religious and political power,[4] in order to serve us in the power of love. We see it as He touched lepers, blessed prostitutes and ate with the "wrong crowd." This is love from above. But He gives it to us – to share – right here on earth.

This is *revolutionary* love that rocks the foundations of the world. So revolutionary it got Jesus killed. Why was His love so upsetting? Because it set people free. Free from hypocritical religious leaders and free from oppressive Roman rulers. It loosened the grip of Roman

---

[3] II Corinthians 5:20
[4] Matthew 4:1-11

control and it redirected popular loyalty away from the Jewish religious leaders. These people killed Jesus because His love upset the balance of power.

Then there were the ordinary people who chanted, "Crucify Him, crucify Him!"[5] Why did they turn on Jesus? Why did they reject His love? Because they didn't understand His kingdom. When it came to life and death politics, they chose to support Barabbas, a political "revolutionary" and murderer, rather than Jesus Christ, the true revolutionary and lover.

The people didn't understand the "new order" of His kingdom, or the Shalom peace it offers. His policy of non-violence disappointed them. They didn't recognize love's power over politics.

MAKING WAVES, NOT SONGS

True love is still misunderstood today. You can turn on the radio, and hear the world singing about "love, sweet love." But the problem is they're singing about *natural* love. This is romantic, sentimental, *self-seeking* and *self-gratifying* love. This is love that expects love in return. This love is for *my* children, *my* family, *my* friends, *my* group, *my* country and people like *me*.[6] This is the love "that makes the world go around."

In contrast, God's *supernatural* love "turns the world upside down." It breaks the "me-barrier," and says, "*we're* in this together!" It knows we're only as rich as our poorest member, only as strong as our weakest link. This is the

---

[5] Mark 15:11-15
[6] Luke 6:32

"color-blind" love of the Good Samaritan,[7] which affirms the value of *every* person, whether woman or child, old or disabled, minority or enemy. This is love that reaches out to orphans, widows and even prisoners with a gentle, helping hand.[8]

This love is also "tough love," which exposes and confronts sin, and calls people to account for their own good. It cares enough to say how destructive adultery, divorce, fornication and other sinful acts really are.[9] It cares enough to tell people the truth about their "human condition," and their need of Jesus. For this reason it's "pro-life" love that makes waves.

And these waves of love don't stop with the issue of abortion. These waves seek to cover the world with justice, equality and mercy. They stir up questions from our murkiest depths, such as, "Can I possibly oppose abortion, yet rationalize wars that murder thousands? Is my personal lifestyle 'pro-life' toward struggling immigrants, unwanted babies and starving children in the third world? Can I be 'pro-life' and not care about dying AIDS patients?"

These are *God's* waves, which have always sought to lift the poor, hungry, and persecuted out of their misery, and crashed judgement down upon the rich, arrogant and hard-hearted people who bury their heads in luxury.[10] These waves of love were demonstrated in Old Testament times by the year of Jubilee.

---

[7] Luke 10:30-37
[8] James 1:27, Matthew 25:42-45
[9] Matthew 5:32
[10] Luke 1:46-53, 6:20, also see prophets, esp. Amos.

What is Jubilee? In His first public message, Jesus said, "The Spirit of the Lord is upon me...to proclaim the favorable year of the Lord."[11] This "favorable year" was a reference to God's year of Jubilee, a celebration (every 50 years) designed to erase all debts, free all slaves, and *start over* with land distribution for all![12] God had ordained this loving cycle of grace to break the grip of greed and oppression among those who had gained advantage over others. For most people Jubilee was good news!

But for those who held the strings of power, nothing could be worse. It stripped them of privilege and status and economic dominance. It called them to surrender power to others, and to become equals again. It called them to participate in God's gracious "kingdom economy." And so it made waves.

KINGDOM DIPLOMACY

As a prince or princess in God's family, you too are called to be an ambassador and wave-maker. Your "home country" is God's heavenly kingdom. Your loyalty and allegiance is to God, not to your ethnic or economic group, your nation or your city. As such, you're a "foreigner" in the world, sent by your Father to personally represent Him, to extend His policy of love and Jubilee. You're called to *share* what you've received, not selfishly hoard or stockpile it. You've been authorized to do this in Jesus' name, through

---

[11] Luke 4:18-19
[12] Leviticus 25, Deuteronomy 15, Jeremiah 34:18, Ezekiel 45:7-9, 46:16-18

the power of the Holy Spirit, in concert with your brothers and sisters everywhere.

Like every ambassador, you're caught between conflicting interests. You know and love the fallen people in your family, your neighborhood, your school and your workplace, and you want to live in peace with them. You don't want to make waves, or enemies, if at all possible. But you also know they need Jesus, and that they're rebelling against God's truth and love, as long as they reject Him. You know you're called to represent and introduce His upside-down kingdom. And this *can* make waves – and require diplomacy.

Diplomacy is hard work. By its very definition, it involves tension, conflict, patience and charm. Christians don't always understand this. But we must understand that our calling to be "in the world, but not *of* the world" isn't an easy one. Salt can sting. Light can expose. Like Jesus, we're called to walk between this present, fallen age and the perfect age to come. And like Him, we catch a lot of flak there!

As a result, we're tempted to run away and *hide* among Christians, or stay and *compromise* among nonbelievers. But we must not do either. These are lose-lose-lose situations. People in the world lose because they don't encounter Christ. You lose because your spiritual integrity falls apart. And God loses because He can't bless the world through you.

This is critical to understand. God's mission is to bless every person and nation in the world, through you and me, as members of His Royal Family. This blessing began with God's promise to Abraham,[13] it was fulfilled in Christ, and it flows through us.

Not long ago, I heard a story from international evangelist Luis Palau that helps us catch a vision for this mission of blessing. He told of two business partners living just outside of Washington D.C., who happen to be longtime friends and Christian brothers. Each year their families get together to celebrate Thanksgiving, and they try to invite someone who would otherwise be "left out in the cold." This one particular Thanksgiving they invited the ambassador from Libya.

The ambassador came and ate turkey, watched football and enjoyed their company. He was deeply blessed by their hospitality. When it was time to leave, he told the men, "If ever I can return this blessing, please let me know."

Months later, the business partners were planning a Middle Eastern business trip, and asked the ambassador if he might arrange a meeting with president Khadaffi, during their visit. The ambassador said he would try, although he was skeptical about the prospects. But sure enough, he called back to report that Khadaffi had agreed to a 15 minute meeting.

When the two men finally met with the infamous dictator and terrorist, things became tense. Their time together had just about expired, when one of our brothers asked if he might pray for the president before leaving. His partner cringed in fear. But Khadaffi considered, then conceded. A prayer would be alright. So our brother stood up, moved to lay a hand on the president's shoulder, and

---

[13] Genesis 12:3

began praying for God's Spirit and blessing to fall on Khadaffi, his family, and his nation. When he finished, tears were streaking Khadaffi's face. Suddenly Khadaffi barked a command to his guards, and they raced out of the room. "Oh, no!" The cringing partner thought to himself. "We're going to die!"

The guards quickly returned, but with a TV camera crew, not a firing squad, in tow. Khadaffi asked the praying brother if he would mind praying *again*, this time for the camera! He explained that he'd never received such a blessing, and wanted to preserve it. And so the brother prayed another blessing in the name of Jesus.

Needless to say, our brothers left that office very relieved, and praising God! And the last they heard, that video clip of prayer was being shown on Libyan television, when broadcasting began each morning!

Isn't that amazing? Yes, these brothers are "full-time" children of God and ambassadors for Christ. They're not "professionals," they simply *profess* Jesus! They're not "in the ministry," they just *minister*. They share *God's* ministry of blessing, in the name of Jesus! Their life in the Holy Spirit naturally *produces* ministry. This is "standard operating procedure" in God's kingdom!

Are you starting to realize that <u>you're a child of God 24 hours a day, seven days a week?</u> Do you know that God's love can pour into every nook and cranny of your life? That God wants His wave of love to touch *every person* you meet? It's true!

As a prince or princess in His kingdom, your life is 100% for God! Wherever you walk is holy ground, because God's Spirit is in you! Please catch this vision.

I'm reminded of a husband and wife I read about recently, who give away a free product or service every day in their business, to express God's Jubilee spirit. They never know when or what it will be, they just sense God's leading, and go with it. Naturally, this has given them quite a reputation with customers! But it's also given them a daily opportunity to tell someone about God's unmerited gift of grace, Jesus Christ. Their lives are overflowing with Jubilee. They represent a foreign kingdom and a loving Father.

And so do you. You're a graceful prince or princess living among desperate, fearful, oppressed and addicted people. You have so much to share with them, if nothing more than a prayer or Shalom blessing! Oh, how people need the grace and love of God. How they need to be touched by the Holy Spirit working through you.

And don't forget to STOP, LOOK and LISTEN. As an ambassador, you can receive *specific* guidance from God, as well as the general policy guidelines of love and Jubilee we've been talking about here. This means we need to embrace God's ways <u>and</u> keep our ears open!

This has been helpful to me in relieving my sometimes false burden for the poor. I've grown comfortable talking and praying with street people, for instance, and am usually willing to give them food or money. I know our Father's heart for such people is full of mercy.

But I also know I can't possibly minister to everyone in need. And I know that helping some people can actually *hinder* God's "tough love" treatment for them. So I've learned to listen to His voice, through the Holy Spirit. "Should I stop and talk with this person, Father?" I ask. "Do you want me to give to this person, or would it do more harm than good?"

His answers (or impressions) give me guidance and wisdom, and keep me from overextending myself. This process applies to many other "diplomatic" decisions and encounters, as well.

FAMILY OF FOOLS, CROWN OF THORNS

We must never forget that our Father's kingdom is a *foreign* kingdom. This means we can look strange, alien, even foolish in the eyes of the world, when we represent Him. This also means that our crowns can have thorns in them.

"Has not God made foolish the wisdom of the world?" Wrote Paul.[14] He was referring to the suffering and death of Jesus Christ, which gave us victory and life. He was referring to a conquering hero who rode a donkey, history's greatest leader, who washed the feet of His followers. He was talking about the ruler who favored women and children over the high and mighty, the "loser" who was beaten and mocked. He was talking about the One who was nailed to a criminal's cross, then tucked away in a tomb. The prince of fools who, in the world's eyes, failed in His mission. He summed it up this way.

"God has chosen the foolish things of the world
to confound the wise, and the weak things of the
world to shame the strong."[15]

---

[14] I Corinthians 1:20
[15] I Corinthians 1:27

Here we go again! God's kingdom is upside-down and backwards. When insulted, we "turn the other cheek."[16] When hated, we love. When cursed, we bless. When cut off in traffic, we forgive! Why do we do such foolish and "meek" things? Because we know that "tit-for- tat" and "eye-for-an-eye" responses leave everybody blind.

The "natural," fallen response is to slap, hate and curse back. But because of God's wisdom in Christ, we know that these responses always escalate. We know that slaps become punches, punches become rocks, rocks become bombs, and then all hell breaks loose. People are maimed, raped, tortured and killed. It's called war, and it's something Adam's family specializes in.

As children of God, we're called to break these "natural" patterns of behavior. We're called to come with the opposite spirit. Love for hate, blessing for curse, "foolishness" for pride. This policy is risky. Forgiveness can be "taken advantage of." Grace can be abused. Generosity can look "wasteful." Like Jesus, who's own family first thought He was crazy,[17] we'll probably be misunderstood. Yet, this is our Father's way, and it's the only way to change the world. Paul wrote,

> "Be imitators of God, as beloved children, and walk in love, just as Christ also loved you, and gave Himself up for us."[18]

---

[16] Matthew 5:29
[17] Mark 3:21
[18] Ephesians 5:1-2

How does this kind of love practically become part of your life? The same way "rest" faith and God's power do. Remember? It comes down to confessing, yielding and receiving, or stopping, looking and listening. You *confess* you don't possess this graceful, courageous love. But you trust your Father has it to share with you, so you *yield* to Him.

You then *receive* His supernatural, wave-making love. It casts out your "natural" fear, and replaces it with Shalom peace. It flows, like every other good thing, from the Father, through you and into the world – turning it upside down. See how that works?

Please stop a moment, and read these paragraphs again, just to let them sink in.

Do you understand that you can't manufacture this risky, courageous love on your own? Do you grasp how God's love must first fill you, before it can overflow from you? (I John 4:19 says, "We love because He first loved us.) And do you see how simply you can be filled, just by asking? I hope so.

Unfortunately, once this supernatural love starts filling you, you can rub the world the "wrong" way. You can ask "strange" questions and take "wierd" stands.

If you're a cop, maybe you *bless* criminals. If you're a coach, maybe you *praise* your worst athletes. If you work for a jerk boss, maybe you do it *joyfully*, as unto the Lord.[19] If you're a wife, maybe you *submit* to your husband, and if you're a husband, maybe you actually *serve* your wife![20] If you're a lawyer, maybe you even *pray* for your opponents!

---

[19] Ephesians 6:7
[20] Ephesians 5:22-29

The creative wave-making possibilities are unlimited when you receive God's love and represent His kingdom.

And so are the costs. We can't forget that people outside the kingdom are in the dark. The world is sick. So if you walk in love, imitating Christ, you'll probably take your beatings and be called a fool along the way. Your crown has thorns.

But that's okay. It's better to be a loving fool for Christ, than a dying sucker for the world. Our Father's supernatural, and sometimes foolish love offers true life, blessing and revolution. We need to affirm this love, and encourage each other to embrace it, because it's Royal Family policy. Here's a prayer to help you.

> Thank you, Abba, Father, for your love
> from above. Thank you for your Jubilee
> spirit of grace and mercy. Please fill me
> up with these awesome things, so I can
> overflow and make some waves! Let me
> live as your ambassador, as a "fool" for
> Christ. In Jesus' name I pray. Amen.

CHAPTER TEN

Family Business

"Go into all the world and preach the gospel."
– Mark 16:15

The young prophet was holding a scribbled note in his hand, as he read. The message had come to him the night before as he prayed, and was intended for me.

Like most real prophecy, it confirmed several things about my life and ministry, that only God could know. It affirmed God's calling and love for me, too. It then concluded with the memorable words, "You take care of my business, and I'll take care of yours."

What did this mean? I figured it was pretty simple. God's business is church ministry, right? So the message was obvious. If I pursued ministry, He would take care of my needs. Fair enough.

But later I had to wonder if it was all so clear cut. After all, what is our Father's business??

As I thought about it, I realized you could say His business is *manufacturing*, or "disciple-making,"[1] where people are newly created to follow in the way of Christ. Or you could say it's *restoration*, where fallen people are made upright in Christ.[2] But I came to the conclusion that God's primary business is *adoption*.

---

[1] Matthew 28:19
[2] II Corinthians 5:17

Yes, our Father operates a worldwide adoption agency, and He employs us to see that it expands!

Our job description is simple. We're to tell our fallen family "relatives" how they can join us in God's family. That's it. Simple and straightforward. "Preaching the gospel" is simply sharing the GOOD NEWS of Royal Family adoption!

We tell people about Jesus, who came to rescue them from the bondage of sin. We tell them how He died to set them free, and rose to empower them. We tell them about the kingdom and the Father's love – and about becoming princes and princesses. We tell them to believe!

WORD-OF-MOUTH ADVERTISING

God has gifted some members of our family with the special ability to do this job. In business they're known as salespeople. But in the kingdom they're known as evangelists. They're the growth-oriented extroverts, who are forever closing adoption "deals" for Christ! (And they're the ones who think we should all go door-to-door!)

Evangelists work to remind us that people "out there" are *blind* and *lost* and *dying* without Jesus. They remind us that our Father's love is good news for *all people*. And they remind us to not keep it a secret! "Good news is for sharing," they tell us. And they're right.

Our Father's business is a "word-of-mouth" operation. It's not driven by hi-tech communications, slick advertising or great entertainment. In fact we fool ourselves when we think these things are necessary to "compete" for the hearts and minds of people. The truth is, <u>there is no</u>

competition for God's love, forgiveness and adoption! We need only demonstrate and communicate it the "old fashioned way." And that's person to person.

Today's most sophisticated marketing experts know the supremacy of this "word of mouth," or testimonial, advertising. Film studios, for instance, love to have big advertising budgets to spend on TV, radio and print promotion. But they like "word-of-mouth" advertising even more.

Nothing can match one excited filmgoer telling a friend, neighbor or co-worker about a good film. This simple, grass-roots communication can turn a low-budget "sleeper" like *Chariots of Fire*, into a box-office hit and Academy Award winner. Word-of-mouth advertising is the most effective way to assure growth in the marketplace.

So why is Christianity slipping in the market, when measured by church membership and attendance? One reason is because we're not doing our job with "word-of-mouth" advertising. We expect the "professionals" to get this work done for us. But this is impossible. They don't know the people we know. They don't go where we go. They don't enjoy our credibility or circle of influence.

No, the job is ours to do. But are we doing it? Are we sharing the good news? Are we telling people how amazing "amazing grace" really is? Are we singing, "I once was lost, but now I'm found" with conviction? Generally, the answer is "no."

Why aren't we spreading the word? I believe it comes back to the reality of our adoption. Is it real for us? Have we felt the Father's embrace, through the Holy Spirit?

Are we overflowing with His love? These are the key questions.

When we can answer "yes," we won't rely on evangelism tracts or TV stations. The love of Christ will force the good news right out of our mouths![3] We'll testify as real "witnesses" who have *seen* God's liberation and power. We'll have something personal to "sell."

"NONE OF YOUR BUSINESS"

Unfortunately, many of us are listening to a lie. Do you know what I'm talking about? I'm talking about the voice that tells you to be quiet about Jesus. The voice that says, "Religion is a *personal* matter, so don't bother people with your views." The voice that says, "Another person's spiritual life is none of your business!"

That voice is not the Father's voice, I can assure you. It's the voice of timidity, which generates fear about making waves, offending others or getting involved. It's the voice of doubt that questions whether Jesus really is "*the* way, *the* truth and *the* life."[4]

This is the same old voice that whispers, "People are 'basically good.'" It insists people are "perfectly healthy" without the Great Physician.

I'm constantly battling this lying voice, as I see people who apparently "have it all," but don't have Jesus. The voice says, "See, their life is great. There's no need for Jesus, adoption, or any of that jazz!" A spirit of timidity begins to dampen my flame for Christ. I become doubtful

---

[3] Acts 4:20 and II Corinthians 5:14
[4] John 14:6

and weak, and begin to falter as a witness.

But then, by God's grace, I remember the truth that, "God has not given us a spirit of timidity, but one of power and love and sound judgment."[5]   My heart swells with power to overcome timidity, and with the Father's love to reach out. My sound judgment returns, and I KNOW people are dying without Jesus. God's Spirit fills me with boldness, so that I, like Paul, can proclaim,

> "I am not ashamed of the gospel, for it is
> the power of God for salvation to everyone
> who believes."[6]

Another lie that can hold back our word-of-mouth message is that, "People already know about Jesus and adoption – they know the whole deal! "

But the truth is, they don't! From what I've discovered, people are ignorant of the basic gospel. It's been so distorted, people think they're either too "bad" for Jesus to accept, or too "good" to need Him at all. But either way, they don't understand the message, or how it applies to them. They desperately need to hear the simple truth. And that's where you and I fit in.

K.I.S.S.!

As we communicate the good news of our Father's business, we need to keep it simple. Perhaps you've heard

---

[5] II Timothy 1:7
[6] Romans 1:16

business people say, "Keep it simple, stupid." (Thus, the acronym, K.I.S.S.) They know the power of simplicity. And so should we.

I can remember an incident a couple of years ago, that demonstrates what I mean. I was in Chicago participating in one of evangelist Leighton Ford's leadership conferences, and was turned loose to minister in Cook County Hospital one evening. As I walked the corridors of that depressing place, listening for our Father's voice of guidance, I had several powerful encounters with people. But the most powerful was also the simplest.

As I passed one room, I was prompted to stop and look in. What I saw stunned me. A young man of about twenty was lying there on a bed with half his face swollen beyond anything I'd ever seen. It was monstrous. After taking a moment to process my shock, I asked, "Hey, you wanna hear about Jesus?"

He nodded weakly, grunting that it was okay. So I sat down next to him and explained the simple truth. "We're all messed up when we don't have a relationship with God," I said. "But Jesus came to get us hooked up right with Him. He loves us and wants to help us get our lives straightened out. Would you like that?" I asked.

He nodded "yes." "Would you like to give your life to Jesus?" I asked. Again he nodded "yes."

And so I led him in prayer. He accepted Jesus right there on the spot. It was almost too simple!

It was so simple, in fact, that it worried me. So I asked whether he had ever accepted Jesus before, thinking it might just be a "rededication."

But he assured me he'd never responded before. I told him how radically different his new life would be, if he chose to live in the kingdom. And he accepted that. I told him he needed to get a Bible, and really dig into it. He understood that, too.

I finally learned that he came from a family full of Christians, and that his time had simply come! It was that simple. And so I left him, praising God for His simple ways.

Now, most of the time we're not roving hospital wards, looking to evangelize. Most of us aren't called to that kind of ministry. But even so, simplicity is the key to sharing what we know from personal experience. I've casually shared the gospel with people at the gym, at CPR classes, even at traffic school!

It's not a big deal. We just need to remember that people don't need our *theology* as much as our "I was blind, now I see!"[7]

Your testimony isn't quite so dramatic? You weren't miraculously rescued out of drugs or adultery or prison? That's okay. You were still rescued.

If you take a good look at your life "B.C.," you'll find plenty of bondage. Maybe you were *blind* to your own sin, and bound by self-righteousness. Maybe you were addicted to "success." Maybe you were a slave to appearances. Just browse through the fallen family traits discussed back in chapter one, and pinpoint the ones that described you.

Think about what God rescued you out of. Then realize that other people around you are trapped in the same

---

[7] John 9:25

shackles today. They need to hear about your deliverance, because they need the same thing. They need to hear testimony from a real witness – YOU!

Hopefully the fruits of your life will lend supporting evidence to your testimony. Hopefully others will see genuine signs of your adoption into God's Royal Family, such as mercy, holiness and love. Hopefully they'll see *Christ in you,* the hope of glory![8]

The simple truth is this. As an adopted child of God, you can share the most important thing in the universe. You can tell of Jesus, your kinsman redeemer, who set you free. You can tell of your Abba, Father's forgiveness, love and adoption. You can tell people about your Father's business of adoption, knowing that He wants a full house.[9]

So please don't sweat the big "E-word" (evangelism). Just live your life in the simplicity of God's love. Don't push and peddle Jesus, like some network marketing pitch. And don't feel guilty if you don't want to preach on streetcorners! Just be open to God's leading and realize people are dying all around you, at work, in your neighborhood, at the store, wherever you go. Look for the outward disguises of their insecurity and pain. Know that God wants to love and heal them, sometimes through you.

So be filled, brother or sister, with power, love and a sound mind – then spread the good news of adoption whenever you can. Here's a prayer to help you.

---

[8] Colossians 1:27
[9] Luke 14:23

Thank you, Abba, Father, for adopting me
as your child, and making me part of your
family. I'm so glad you sent your Son to
rescue me from sin, fear and death. Please
help me to share this good news with others.
Give me simple words, and a willing spirit.
Fill me with your love for others, in Jesus'
wonderful name. Amen.

CHAPTER ELEVEN

Family Feud

"Put on the full armor of God so that you can take
your stand against the devil's schemes." – Ephesians 6:11

"I don't want to fight!" screamed the new recruit, as bullets whistled past his head.

"Too late, pal," his buddy yelled back. "All hell's breaking lose, and we're stuck in the middle of it!"

As children of God, we can say the same thing. We've been adopted into a family at war, and hence, there's no escaping conflict. We can't be "conscientious objectors" or "civilians" in the kingdom. We're called to be *warriors* who fight against an enemy who never stops trying to destroy us.[1]

Who is this enemy? It's Satan (the devil), the one who stole the original blessing of righteousness, peace and joy from Adam and Eve back in the garden. He's the one mentioned over 200 times in scripture, and called the "god of this world,"[2] the "prince of darkness,"[3] the "accuser,"[4] the "oppressor,"[5] the "murderer," and the "father of lies."[6] He's the one who tempted Jesus in the wilderness,[7] was

---

[1] I Peter 5:8
[2] John 14:30
[3] Ephesians 6:12
[4] Revelation 12:10
[5] Isaiah 51:13
[6] John 8:44
[7] Luke 4:1-13

overpowered by Jesus during His ministry,[8] and was conquered by Jesus on the cross.[9]

Yes, Satan was defeated, but he's not finished yet. Make no mistake about it. He still maintains power on earth in the lives of people. He won't be completely wiped out until Jesus comes back to usher in His full and perfect kingdom. Then he'll be cast into the lake of fire.[10] In the meantime, Satan attacks us, forever trying to strip our faith, neutralize our power and compromise our testimony. And if you don't believe it, he's got you right where he wants you!

Many of us are living in this pitifully weak condition. Doubtful and defenseless. We haven't received even "basic training" in spiritual warfare. We haven't gained "intelligence" about enemy operations, or "survival tactics" to overcome them.

But victory is ours if we'll stop long enough to learn about these things. If we will, we'll learn how to be *conquerors* and *overcomers,* through the work of Christ and the power of the Holy Spirit. We'll gain victory on each of Satan's three battlefronts.

1.) THE FLESH

The first battlefront we face is in the mirror. This is where the "old self" looms. You remember that person born into Adam's family? Remember how he or she officially

---

[8] Matthew 12:28
[9] Colossians 2:15, Genesis 3:15
[10] Revelation 19:11-20:10

"died" when you were adopted? Well, that person wants to resurrect!

Although you're no longer *subject* to sin, as a child of God, you still *can* sin. Your sinful nature has been broken, but it hasn't been totally removed yet. This ability to sin, this "old self" of yours, is sometimes called "the flesh."[11]   It hangs around with you until you die, and wants to drag you back into sin, in the meantime.   Your fleshly "old self" literally wages war against God's Spirit in you – your "new self."[12]

As I've been writing this, my kids have interrupted me, our baby has been screaming, I've spoken harshly, lost my temper, and I've felt like wringing somebody's neck! In other words, my fleshly old self has risen up. My frustration and anger are "natural" reactions. And that's just my point. I've been yielding to Satan's power resident in my old and fallen nature.

But this power doesn't have to dominate me. I can kill it off any time by simply changing my mind. Paul wrote, "The mind set on the flesh is death, but the mind set on the Spirit is life and peace."[13] This means I *choose* which way to set my mind. I can yield to my old self, and the death that comes with it, or I can yield to my new self, *alive with God's Spirit*. These choices produce *words and actions* that are life-giving or destructive, depending on which way I go. One choice leads to *victory* over Satan's residual power, the other *surrenders* to it.

---

[11] Romans 7:14
[12] Romans 7:23, Colossians 3:7-15, James 4:1
[13] Romans 8:6

And so when I catch myself flaring up in the flesh, I repent. I turn and ask for Father's help, yielding myself to His Spirit of life and peace. Like a slashing sword,[14] His Spirit kills off my old self and empowers me to react in a new and life-giving way. He raises up Christlikeness in me. He enables me to attend to my kids, quiet the baby, apologize for my words and move with gentleness.

This Spirit-filled response is made easier because I "renew my mind" each day by reading the Bible.[15] Like spiritual soap, it cleans out the old self, and shines up the new. It fosters a healthy mind set on God, more able to obey Paul's helpful words,

> "Whatever is true, whatever is honorable, whatever is right, whatever is pure, whatever is lovely, whatever is admirable – if anything is excellent or praiseworthy – let your mind dwell on these things."[16]

Yes, the battle between your new and old self is fought in your mind. You can yield to the Spirit, or to the flesh. It's almost like flipping a mental switch one way or the other between two opposite personalities – one noble, the other carnal. As shown on the following page, the choice is yours.[17]

---

[14] Ephesians 6:17
[15] Romans 12:2
[16] Philippians 4:8
[17] Ephesians 2:2-3, Galatians 5:19-26, Colossians 3:5-14

CHILD OF GOD (New Self in the Spirit)	**CHILD OF WRATH** (Old Self in the flesh)
Loving	Selfish, jealous, prejudiced
Joyful	Resentful, angry, bothered
Peaceful	Hostile, divisive, worried
Patient	Pushy, anxious, driven
Kind	Mean, arrogant, slanderous
Good	Cynical, perverted, greedy
Faithful	Unreliable, disobedient
Gentle	Gruff, abusive, obnoxious
Self-controlled	Erratic, indulgent, lustful

2.) THE WORLD

You can look around and see the second battlefield. It's called the world. And Satan controls it by controlling most of the people in it. This accounts for the incredible current you feel pulling at you like an ocean riptide. We call it "peer pressure," when we talk about kids. But no matter what our age, Satan pressures us to *conform* to the fashions, trends and movements of the world. This pressure can take the form of Naziism, as it did in Hitler's Germany, or consumerism, as it does in modern America.

These subtle forces erode our spiritual defenses little by little and sweep us away from our Father. We're usually too busy to ask or think where they're taking us or where they came from. These forces can look like "conveniences," or "advances" or "progress," too. They tempt us to go along like children who say, "Everyone is doing it!" And so we get swept along with the world – right over a cliff!

Back in chapter six, we talked about the *trouble* Jesus promised us in the world.[18] Remember? He said we belonged to His kingdom, not to the world.[19] He said the world would *hate us*, because of our identity in Him.[20] But how soon we forget!

Satan is amazingly seductive. Just go to the store, page through a magazine, or watch TV, and you'll see what I mean. He bombards us with alluring images that ultimately erode our life of faith. He lures us with false promises and wishful fantasies. He expertly pushes our "buttons" of fear and insecurity, always driving us toward idolatry, which is our love of – or interest in – *anything* more than God. Our idols can be cars, clothes, careers, hobbies, travels, homes, celebrities, ministries, even families!

I can remember one night when I was praying for more of God's power in my life, when He confronted me about idolatry. But I couldn't figure out what it was. So I kept putting likely candidates on the altar. My worldly

---

[18] John 16:33
[19] John 15:19
[20] Luke 21:17

ambition. My love of money. My ministry. You name it. I dragged them out and asked Him to remove them. But I sensed Him saying, "No, we've dealt with these before. You need to surrender something else."

After repeating this process some more, I finally stopped and asked what the idol was. I was stumped.

When God whispered, "Suzi and the kids," I was shocked. "My family?" I asked in disbelief. "Yes," He confirmed.

So I surrendered my wife and children to Him, one by one. And as I did, I died a thousand deaths. Tears surfaced from depths I didn't know existed. I wept as if I was at their actual funerals, it was that emotional to me. Somehow I was letting go of them and abandoning myself to God alone.

Of course I had no idea they had become my "first love," in place of Jesus. But sure enough, they had. And as I released them, God's blessings flowed.

I soon felt a healthier, less compulsive love for my wife and kids. I became free to love and appreciate them the way my heavenly Father does. I was no longer clinging to them or dependent upon them. God's love filled the place idolatry had held in my heart, and released new power into my life. Praise God!

The point I want to make is this. Satan operates behind the scenes of the world, tempting and seducing us. He looks for ways to misdirect our love – away from God. He wants to attract our love and loyalty to other things – even "good" things like families, careers, countries, etc. And his tactics are state-of-the-art.

As an experienced advertising copywriter, I know how artful this worldly science has become. In the world, Satan goes for the jugular vein through psychological research and market testing! He's the master of manipulation who knows all your weaknesses, and just how to exploit them. (Notice how "sex sells?")

He paints a captivating picture of "the good life," then makes you feel foolish or "wierd" if you don't lust after it. He insists that you conform yourself to worldly "role models" rather than to Jesus Christ. He demands that you "play by the rules" and "go with the flow."

He's also the one escalating the competition, raising the stakes and promoting the win-at-all-costs attitude in the world. He's the one pushing the pace faster and faster, the technology further and further, and just about everything out of control! The tide is fierce. The pressure to conform is almost overwhelming. He wants you to bow to the world.

This is why the Bible says, "Do not be conformed to this world."[21] "Do not love the world, nor the things in the world. If anyone loves the world, the love of the Father is not in him."[22] This is why it reminds us, "Do you not know that friendship with the world is hostility toward God?"[23] And this is why Jesus warned against succumbing to the "cares of this world."[24]

As children of God, we're called to *overcome* the world,[25] not become molded by it. How do we do this? By

---

[21] Romans 12:2
[22] I John 2:15
[23] James 4:4
[24] Matthew 13:22
[25] I John 5:4-5

dwelling in the peace of Jesus Christ[26] through the Holy Spirit. By standing in God's truth, which exposes the deceptions of the world. By knowing God gives us "x-ray vision" to see things as they really are.

As we walk in the Spirit listening to our Father, we're able to look *behind* pretty pictures and false advertisements – to the truth. We examine the "heart of the matter," not just the appearance. We ask childlike "why" questions about the world around us. "Why are we doing this?" We ask. "Why are we buying that?" "Why does everyone think this is true, or good, or right?"

In other words, we question the assumptions and statements of the world, holding them up like x-ray negatives to the Light of the World, Jesus Christ. We abide in His word and hence, we know the truth.[27] And the truth sets us free from the world's attractive – and always deceptive – grip.

Much of the "stress" we complain about in the world today can be avoided by asking these simple questions. "Why am I so busy?" "Why am I so distracted?" "Why are my relationships so superficial, my communication so poor? Why am I so frustrated and depressed?"

God's answers often reveal that we're being swept along with the world. We're chasing false illusions, setting worldly goals, pursuing false hopes. We're wasting precious time in front of televisions, sacrificing valuable peace near blaring radios and chatter. We're trying to do too many unimportant things, while ignoring the truly important.

---

[26] John 16:33
[27] John 8:32

To overcome the world, we must expose it, and deal ruthlessly with it – by turning off the TV, pitching those magazines, staying out of those stores, or bars, or whatever it takes! We must understand how violently the world opposes the kingdom and our relationship with God. We must recognize that Satan wants to squeeze us into the world's destructive mold of idolatry. Conform us to its false images. Pull us away from God's perfect will.

So be alert. Ask questions. Don't be fooled by appearances. Call out for the x-ray eyes of Jesus. Pray for God's wisdom and revelation, and for His power to overcome.

3.) SATAN

Our last battleground is direct conflict with Satan and his evil spirits, or demons. While many people dismiss their existence as mere superstition, and even treat them with humor, we must treat evil spirits very seriously. Although they're invisible to our eyes, they're as real as any bacteria, and as destructive as any plague.

The first thing Jesus did in His ministry was resist Satan's efforts to pervert His mission.[28] Soon afterward He began His ministry of deliverance, casting demons out of people afflicted in various ways.[29] He said, "If I drive out demons by the Spirit of God, then the kingdom of God has come upon you."[30]   As the Son of God, Jesus had total

---

[28] Mark 4:1-11
[29] Luke 4:33-35, Mark 5:1-12, 9:14-29
[30] Matthew 12:28

authority over demons, and as adopted children of God so do we. Jesus gave this authority to His first followers,[31] and to us, saying,

> "These signs will accompany those who
> have believed: in My name they will cast
> out demons..."[32]

We see how this authority works in Acts 16:16-18, when Paul delivers a bothersome fortuneteller from a spirit of divination, by commanding the spirit out of her in the name (and authority) of Jesus Christ. Jesus' mighty name, exalted by the Father above every other name,[33] is the key to our victory over Satan.

As members of God's Royal Family, we have shared in the death and resurrection of Jesus Christ, which "disarmed the (demonic) rulers" and "triumphed over them."[34] Evil spirits recognize the power and authority of His name when spoken by us in faith. They must obey.

How do we recognize demons? How do they operate? How do we get rid of them and steer clear of them?

Demons are recognized supernaturally, through the gift of discernment (as in chapter eight's examples), or when demons identify themselves in direct conversation.[35] I remember speaking to a demon named Lonesome Soldier

---

[31] Luke 9:1, 10:19
[32] Mark 16:17
[33] Philippians 2:9
[34] Colossians 2:15
[35] Mark 5:9

once who had possession of a "mentally ill" bag lady living on the street.

Demons can also be identified through physical manifestations like anger, fear, convulsions and vomiting when confronted by the name or presence of Jesus Christ.[36] And still other times, evil spirits are discovered only after Spirit-led ministry exposes strongholds rooted in a person's unforgiveness, bitter judgments or unconfessed areas of sinful activity.

How do demons operate? For starters, they enter "open doors" of doubt, rebellion, bitterness, immorality and occultic activity (i.e. witchcraft, sorcery, astrology, etc.). They seek to blind people to the glory of Jesus Christ,[37] and pervert God's good purposes for them. Their mission is to deceive and destroy in every possible way.

I'm convinced that many witches and occultic prac- titioners have been twisted away from their true callings in God's kingdom by demonic assault. Satan empowers them with his own deceptive "spiritual gifts" and hinders them from serving the true and living God. Not surprisingly, some of the most gifted Christians I know endured years of intense Satanic oppression before being liberated by Christ.

Satan starts by gaining "toe-holds" through our wrongful thoughts, false beliefs and bad attitudes, espe- cially unforgiveness. This opens the door to spirits of deception, which gain "footholds" through our sinful pat- terns and harmful addictions. Ultimately Satan controls us through dominating "strongholds" of ever-deepening bond-

---

[36] Mark 9:14-29
[37] II Corinthians 4:3-4

age.

Before he was executed, serial sex killer Ted Bundy confessed how occasional exposure to soft-core pornography grew over the years into obsessive and hard-core sexual addiction. This addiction led to uncontrollable urges to "act out" perverted and murderous behaviors. He explained that the power and personality of his bondage seemed demonic.

Satan and his demons forever seek to distort the truth, usually *mixing* what's true, *including scripture*,[38] with what's false. This is why religious cults like the Mormons, Moonies and Jehovah's Witnesses continue to flourish. Undiscerning people open spiritual doors and demons rush right in, steering people away from simple faith in Jesus Christ.

How do we get rid of demons? First of all, <u>we make</u> <u>*sure* we're dealing with demons</u>. This isn't the place for whimsical hunches or guesswork. We need revelation, either by the Holy Spirit directly, through a fellow Christian with the gift of discernment, or by the evil spirit manifesting itself. Demons can be identified by specific name[39] or by general recognition.[40] But either way, revelation is required so that we don't mistake ordinary emotional, spiritual or physical problems for Satanic possession or oppression.

Let me repeat this point of caution. This is no place for guesswork. Deliverance ministry is no game. So be cautious and be sure.

Secondly, we *take authority* in Jesus' name. We remember the scripture that says, "Greater is He who is in us,

---

[38] Luke 4:10-11
[39] Mark 5:9
[40] Acts 16:18

then he who is in the world."[41] We remember the authority given to us by Jesus, confident that,

> "The weapons we fight with are not the weapons of the world. On the contrary, they have divine power to demolish strongholds."[42]

Every demonic stronghold is subject to the name of Jesus. By our faith in His death and resurrection, we're authorized to use His divinely powerful name to *bind* and *cast out* evil spirits. We bind them to silence or to immobilize them."[43] And this enables us to cast them out without unnecessary physical or verbal activity.[44] We simply bind them and cast them out – commanding them to *stay* out[45] – in Jesus' name.

This process can be time-consuming and exhausting however, because demons challenge our faith,[46] question our authority[47] and resist expulsion. Sometimes a person is unwilling or "not ready" to be delivered, too. And sometimes there are numerous spirits to contend with (Mary Magdalene was delivered from seven demons).[48]

---

[41] I John 4:5
[42] II Corinthians 10:4
[43] Matthew 12:29, 16:19,
[44] Luke 4:35
[45] Mark 9:25, Matthew 12:43-45
[46] Mark 9:17-19, 23
[47] Acts 9:13-17
[48] Mark 16:9

For these reasons, <u>we should always avoid solo deliverance ministry,</u>[49] <u>and should always seek help from more gifted and experienced brothers and sisters.</u> And we should *always listen to the Holy Spirit* for His guidance and special instruction.[50]

We must remember too, that we battle *Satan*, not the people he's possessed or oppressed. When Peter tried to hinder Jesus' call to the cross, for example, Jesus recognized His true foe. "Get behind me, Satan!"[51] He said. He didn't take it out on Peter.

This reminds us of the need for intercessory prayer, since we struggle not against people but against "spiritual forces of wickedness."[52] We can wage warfare against these spiritual strongholds, breaking chains that keep people out of the kingdom, knowing that most people who receive Christ have someone praying for them. As we are led by the Spirit, we can pray for God to set people free!

And finally, we can resist demons and actually make them flee. How? By submitting to our Father, and standing firm in our faith.

How do we best do this? I suggest we do this by confessing our sins and seeking prayer with brothers and sisters. By repenting and forgiving whenever necessary. By remaining open to our Father's guidance and correction, knowing that He wants to protect us from temptation and

---

[49] Luke 10:17-20, Jesus sent the 70 in pairs, also Matt 18:20
[50] Mark 9:29
[51] Matthew 16:23
[52] Ephesians 6:12

harm. These things *close* doors instead of open them to Satanic assault.

   We gain the strength to resist Satan as we pray and spend time in the scriptures, aligning ourself with our Father's will, as we occupy our minds with the things of God and as we sing praises and thank Him in our hearts. As we *listen*. These practices lead to our faithful obedience, the very thing Satan hates most! It reminds him of Jesus, who obeyed unto death, and who crushed him under our feet![53]

   Now read the last paragraph again, and pretend you're Satan. Would you mind Christians praying and reading and meditating on the word of God? Of course you would! You'd mind it so much you'd try to stop it! And Satan does. Through your rebelling flesh, through the distractions of the world, and through direct assaults, he seeks to kill your faith. He does so by keeping you out of the Bible, out of prayer and out of Christian fellowship. As long as he does, there's no telling how badly he can hurt you.

   So don't let it happen. Be advised. You don't pray and study scripture because it's "the Christian thing to do." You do it to stay healthy and strong! You do it to cover yourself with the "full armor of God."[54] You do it because your spiritual life and relationship with the Father depend upon it. Here's a prayer to help you face the battle.

---

[53] Romans 16:20
[54] Ephesians 6:10-17

Thank You, Abba, Father, for adopting me
and giving me the power to conquer my flesh,
the world and Satan. Give me wisdom, discernment and x-ray vision to see the truth in every
situation. And give me the strength to stand firm
as a warrior. In Jesus' name I pray. Amen.

CHAPTER TWELVE

Family Unity

"This is My commandment, that you love one another, just as I have loved you." – John 15:12

As children of God, we need to remind ourselves that we've been adopted into a spiritual *family*. Not a religious organization, or church denomination, but a family. As such, we belong to God our Father, and are knitted together with millions of brothers and sisters throughout the world. We're joined together in the name of Jesus through the power of the Holy Spirit. We're supposed to be *united in love*.

The apostle Paul was so passionate about Christian unity that he wrote, "As a prisoner for the Lord, I urge you to live a life worthy of the calling you have received. Be completely humble and gentle, be patient, bearing with one another in love. Make every effort to keep the unity of the Spirit through the bond of peace." He continued,

> "There is one body and one Spirit...one Lord, one faith, one baptism, one God and Father of all who is over all and through all and in all."[1]

He knew that unity means *oneness* – he mentioned it *six times* in one sentence! He knew that unity was supposed to be the hallmark of God's Royal Family, in contrast

---

[1] Ephesians 4:1-6

to the division, strife and competition of Adam's fallen family. And he knew that when Jesus prayed for us on the single occasion recorded in scripture, He asked the Father to make us one.[2]   Jesus then prayed,

> "May they (believers) be brought to complete
> unity to let the world know that You sent Me."[3]

Could He be any clearer? No. God's greatest desire for us is unity. It's the one thing capable of convincing the world that He sent His Son. Why is "complete unity" so convincing? Because unity is a miracle.

A HOUSE DIVIDED

Unfortunately, what God intended to be a supernatural wonder has become a natural disaster. Christianity is like a noisy household, full of fussing and fighting, splits, divisions, divorces and runaway children. Outsiders can only shake their heads and keep their distance. We're a disgrace to our Father.

"Any kingdom divided against itself will be ruined," said Jesus, "and a house divided against itself will fall."[4] How tragic it is that these words, originally related to *Satan's* domain, now describe God's kingdom on earth. There are countless Christian movements, sects and denominations today, and there are just as many petty debates between them. Missionary organizations often compete,

---

[2] John 17:21
[3] John 17:23
[4] Luke 11:17

rather than cooperate, while parachurch organizations often foster exclusive, prideful attitudes among their members. All the while, Catholics and Protestants slug it out over the same dividing wall that's existed for centuries. How did God's house become so divided?

Some people would point to the Protestant reformation and Martin Luther, but this would be a mistake. Yes, he sparked a huge breakaway movement from the Roman (Catholic) church in 1517, but this wasn't the church's first breakup by any stretch of the imagination. A couple of centuries earlier, the church endured the Great Schism (i.e. split), a period during which three different Popes operated at the same time!

Controversy and division have been constant elements of Christianity dating back to the first century, when false prophets made the rounds, preaching a "different gospel,"[5] saying, among other things, that Jesus had not come in the flesh. Why have there always been such problems?

I suggest the main reason is that Christians have failed to experience true adoption. We've dragged our fallen family traits into the church, because we haven't entered the "narrow gate" of God's kingdom. We haven't allowed the righteousness, peace and joy of the Holy Spirit to invade our hearts and lower our defenses.

We've played politics and practiced religion, but we haven't experienced the Father's love and approval through intimate relationship. As a result, we've behaved like children of wrath, rather than children of God.

---

[5] Galatians 1:7

RECONCILIATION

In Adam's dysfunctional family, when people divorce or break up they normally cite "irreconcilable differences" as the reason. This is an acceptable explanation for falling apart in the world.

But in God's Royal Family, such "differences" are disasterous and unacceptable. This is true because we've been given the "ministry of reconciliation."[6] We can't just "go our separate ways!" On the contrary, we're called to work out our differences as loving *bridge-builders* and *peace-makers*. We're called to constantly work toward unity, especially among our own brothers and sisters.[7]

You may think this work sounds difficult. But I want you to know it's more than difficult. It's practically *impossible*. No matter how hard we try, we can't do it on our own. Our attitudes, gifts and experiences are too varied. Our viewpoints and expectations are too different. We just don't see eye-to-eye in the church. So how can we come together? We must die.

Like most other good things from God, who makes "all things possible,"[8] unity exists to the extent that we *decrease,* or *die* to ourselves. This is true because *unity is a fruit of the Holy Spirit*, not a product of our human nature. Our old nature says, "I'm a Catholic or Baptist or Methodist or Lutheran. I'm part of this movement, or a follower of that preacher. My views are right, and other Christians are wrong."

---

6 II Corinthians 5:19
7 Matthew 5:9, Galatians 6:10
8 Matthew 19:26

But the Holy Spirit prompts us to say, "I'm a child of God and follower of Christ. I love my brothers and sisters, and want to be united with them through the bond of peace. I want to balance truth with love. I need to listen and learn." Paul promoted this approach, saying,

> "Make my joy complete by being of the
> same mind, maintaining the same love, united
> in spirit, intent on one purpose. Do nothing
> from selfishness or empty conceit, but with
> humility of mind let each of you regard one
> another as more important than yourself."[9]

How can we possibly live this way? Only by having a relationship with our Abba Father. Only by being "imitators of God, as beloved children," who walk in the love Jesus shared with us.[10] Only by dwelling in His spiritual kingdom and surrendering to His perfect will. There is no other way.

Don't you think it's time for this way to become the rule, not the exception, of Christian life? I think so. I believe it's time for God's love, the "perfect bond of unity,"[11] to be released in our hearts and in our churches. I believe this is our Father's will, and that it starts with you and me.

If we say we love our heavenly Father, the Bible says we *must* love each other.[12] Whether we're rich or poor, male or female, black or white, or anything in between. Whether

---

[9] Philippians 2:2-3
[10] Ephesians 5:1-2
[11] Colossians 3:14
[12] I John 4:20

we agree on every theological fine point or not. And whether we attend your modern mega-church or my little old chapel. If we belong to Christ, then you and I are royal co-heirs and fellow ambassadors. We're not loners or self-centered individuals. And we're not judges, either. We're Christ-centered children of God, and we're on the same team!

We're each secure in our Father's love, we know we each have important functions to fulfill, and so we have no need to compete with each other. We share a common, life-giving cause. In fact, we're called to "bear each other's burdens,"[13] "confess our sins one to another,"[14] and "rejoice in the Lord always."[15]

Does this describe your Christian experience? I hope it does. But if it doesn't, I want you to know it can and *should*. Bearing (not *bury*ing) burdens, confessing (not *conceal*ing) sins and rejoicing (yes, rejoicing!) is for real life. Your life and mine. Yes, it can be messy at times, and yes, it can be humbling (and risky) to admit problems and struggles with each other, but that's what God's family is for! Our shared life builds faith and brings healing, and so we rejoice.

Given this mutual love and submission, I say it's time to reach across our organizational boundaries with the right hand of fellowship. At work, at school, in the neighborhood and around the world, we need to get together. It's time for suburban churches to partner with urban churches, to exchange material and spiritual blessings. It's time for

---

[13] Galatians 6:1, I John 3:17
[14] James 5:16
[15] Philippians 4:4

local pastors and priests to meet, listen and pray together, repenting and forgiving and loving, so that Christian unity might invade whole cities!

I say it's time for missionary and parachurch organizations to humbly cooperate and be accountable to each other. It's time for us to obey God and love one another. The world will marvel, and our Father will be glorified, as the barriers fall.

Is this vision far-fetched? Too idealistic? Well, if it is, then so was Jesus. And so was Paul, who wrote,

"As God's chosen people, holy and dearly loved, clothe yourselves with compassion, kindness, humility, gentleness and patience. Bear with each other and forgive whatever grievances you may have against one another. Forgive as the Lord forgave you. And over all these virtues put on love, which binds them all together in perfect unity. Let the peace of Christ rule in your hearts, since as members of one body you were called to peace. And be thankful...Teach and admonish one another with all wisdom, and sing psalms, hymns and spiritual songs with gratitude in your hearts to God. And whatever you do, whether in word or deed, do it all in the name of the Lord Jesus, giving thanks to God the Father through Him."[16]

---

[16] Colossians 3:12-17

Isn't this vision awesome?! As I read the apostle's words I'm completely humbled, yet totally inspired. Just listen to a few of his favorites. Compassion. Kindness. Humility. Gentleness. Patience. Forgiveness. Peace. And gratitude. Even singing!

These are the words – and this is the reality – of Shalom. Remember "heaven on earth" back in the garden? Remember how we talked about "kingdom life?"

Well, this is the life God offers you in His kingdom. Will you live there? Can we live there together? I believe we can.

But it starts with you and me, right here and now, opening ourselves to the love of our Father and the unity of the Spirit, submitting ourselves to one another. Let's pray.

Forgive us, Father, for we have sinned against you. We repent of our pride, jealousy and disobedience. We have shamefully divided your household, and we're sorry. Please help us to love one another as you have loved us. Help us to forgive, rather than judge, and build bridges rather than walls. Heal your family, Abba, Father, so the world might know you sent your Son to save it. Fill us with unity and love, in Jesus' glorious name. Amen!

A Family Plan

"Do not fool yourselves by just listening to His word.
Instead, put it into practice." – James 1:22

So where do we go from here? I have several suggestions, but before I share them, let me draw your attention to the word, "we." This is the key word in the Royal Family. We must move forward *together*, if we're going to get anywhere. My first suggestion therefore, centers on this point.

1.) **Find a Partner**. Jesus sent His followers out to minister and grow together in pairs.[1] I believe this is still God's preferred method of fostering our spiritual growth. If you're married, you already have one kind of "spiritual growth partner." But the partner I'm suggesting is a special friend, normally of the same sex as you. A Christian brother or sister committed to God and to you in a special relationship.

This person can pray with you, hear your confessions, bear your burdens and keep you accountable to the truth. This is so important! You need someone who can see your "blind spots," recognize warning signs, and speak the truth in love to you, from a place of intimacy and trust. A faith partner can provide counsel and inspiration to direct you closer to God. A partner can also encourage you to "live

---

[1] Luke 10:1

by faith" in every part of your life and to seek after God's purposes. A partner can affirm your ministry gifts, too. You can even have more than one spiritual growth partner, to meet different needs or interests.

But the bottom line is that a faith partner will help you grow as a child of God. Without one, you'll probably mature slowly, if at all. So ask your Father who you should develop a special relationship with. Ask that He provide you with just the right partner. And once He does, be faithful to water your relationship with that person. Then grow together!

2.) **Share the vision**. I've written this book to help you catch a vision for your life as a child of God. It's not a "new" vision, or "my" vision. It's God's vision given to us through Jesus Christ, and expressed to us by Paul and other biblical writers centuries ago. I've only dusted it off like an old family album, to share among brothers and sisters. Now you can share it, too.

I felt impressed to keep this book short and simple so that you could read it and share it easily. Can you think of any Christians – or potential Christians – who might benefit from reading it? Think of family members, neighbors, co-workers and other people around town, including your pastor or priest. Why not pass a copy of this book along to them? You don't need to be pushy, just tell them they might enjoy it. Practice some of that word-of-mouth advertising we discussed in chapter nine! Then follow up and talk about it. But whatever you do, pass the good news around the family.

3.) **Study it close**. Ever notice how children like to hear the same story read to them, over and over again? My kids do this and memorize every page! They've shown me how repetition works in learning, and I want to remind you. Read this book again. If not word for word, then at least by repeating headlines, quotes and prayers. Why not memorize the various headline verses, such as, "Power is perfected in weakness," in chapter eight, or, "In love, God predestined us to adoption through Jesus Christ to Himself," back in chapter three? Why not open your Bible and study the scriptural references in each chapter's footnotes? There are over 250 of them! This will give your reading lasting impact. So study it close.

4.) **Seek His kingdom**. Finally, and most importantly, remember the focal point of Jesus' ministry, the kingdom of God. He came to give you "kingdom life" and relationship with God, the Father. <u>The reality of this life, filled, empowered and guided by the Holy Spirit, is what Christianity is all about!</u>

Please don't settle for anything less. The Bible says, "The work of the righteous is life."[2] I pray you'll receive this life, cultivate it, enjoy it, and spread it around in Jesus' name – to the glory of our Father! Amen.

---

[2] Proverbs 10:16

To Order

additional copies of

Royal Family

_Finding Your Identity and
Purpose in the Kingdom of God_

Send $12.00 per book

(includes tax, shipping and handling)

to:

**ABBA
PRESS**
**3913 Via Cardelina
Palos Verdes, CA 90274**